SO, YOU WANT TO BE AN
ENTREPRENEUR?

Ismail Ahmed

Copyright © 2024 ISMAIL AHMED

All rights reserved. No part of this book may be reproduced in any form without permission from the author or publisher,

Globally Available

ISBN: 978-2-3935-0575-1

Published in Nigeria, 2024
Emphaloz Publishing House

A catalogue record for this book is available at the National Library of Nigeria

TABLE OF CONTENT

PREFACE	*iv*
CHAPTER ONE	*1*
The Spark: Finding Your Why	
CHAPTER TWO	*20*
From Idea To Execution	
CHAPTER THREE	*37*
The Entrepreneurial Mindset: Thinking Big, Starting Small	
CHAPTER FOUR	*52*
Crafting Your Business Plan	
CHAPTER FIVE	*69*
Funding The Dream: How To Secure Resources For Your Business	
CHAPTER SIX	*84*
Building Connections That Matter	
CHAPTER SEVEN	*100*
Scaling Smartly	
CHAPTER EIGHT	*119*
Fail Fast, Learn Faster	
CHAPTER NINE	*134*
The Social Impact Of Entrepreneurship: Giving Back Through Business	
CHAPTER TEN	*152*
Legacy And Longevity	
CHAPTER ELEVEN	*169*
Understanding Legal And Compliance Essentials	
CHAPTER TWELVE	*187*
Wellness And Balance: Thriving Without Burnout	

PREFACE

Entrepreneurship is a thrilling adventure, a journey filled with aspirations, challenges, and moments of transformation. Whether you're in finance, technology, agriculture, fashion, or any other industry, the decision to create something meaningful is one of the boldest choices you can make.

This book isn't about lofty theories or unattainable ideals. It's a collection of lessons, stories, and practical advice as an entrepreneur and observer of countless others. It's designed to speak to anyone and derive actionable directions.

Throughout these pages, you'll find insights to help you uncover your "why," navigate the uncertainties of starting and growing a business, and build something that doesn't just succeed but thrives. My hope is that this book becomes a guide, a friend, and a source of inspiration as you embark on or refine your entrepreneurial path.

So, let's dive in together. The world needs your ideas, your courage, and your determination. Are you ready to begin?

CHAPTER ONE
THE SPARK: FINDING YOUR WHY

Embarking on the journey of entrepreneurship begins with an internal question that is as profound as it is personal: *What drives me?* The answer to this question is the cornerstone of every entrepreneurial venture. It's what propels you forward when obstacles arise, and it's the lens through which you view opportunities and risks. Your motivation acts as the silent engine of your business pursuits, shaping decisions, defining goals, and sustaining you through both the highs and lows.

For some, the allure of entrepreneurship lies in the promise of freedom. The idea of being your own boss, setting your own schedule, and answering no one but yourself is undoubtedly attractive. The thought of charting your own course and breaking free from the confines of traditional employment can feel liberating. Yet, as enticing as this freedom sounds, it comes with its own set of responsibilities and challenges. Freedom in entrepreneurship is not handed to you, but it is earned through discipline, sacrifice, and an unwavering commitment to your vision. It's about taking ownership not only your successes but also your failures.

Others may be driven by a deep-seated desire to solve a problem. Perhaps you've encountered a recurring frustration in your industry or personal life that sparks the thought, *there has to be a better way*. Entrepreneurs are often natural problem-solvers, compelled by a sense of curiosity and innovation. They see inefficiencies not as roadblocks but as opportunities to create solutions. This type of motivation is particularly powerful because it is rooted in a sense of purpose. When you are driven by the need to make a tangible difference whether by improving lives, streamlining processes, or addressing mate needs you are inherently connected to the value your business brings to the world.

For some, the spark to build something of their own comes from observing a gap in the market. These individuals are motivated by opportunity, seeing what others might overlook and having the courage to act on it. Spotting an underserved audience, a niche product, or a growing trend can ignite the entrepreneurial spirit. This type of drive often involves a blend of strategic thinking and foresight, the ability to predict not only what people need now but also what they might want in the future. It's about recognizing potential and having the audacity to claim it before anyone else does.

There are also those whose motivations are more personal and deeply rooted in their life experiences. Perhaps you were raised in a family where entrepreneurial efforts were the foundation of survival and growth. Maybe you watched a parent build something from nothing, instilling in you a sense of pride and determination to follow in their footsteps. Alternatively, your drive might stem from an experience of scarcity or struggle, fueling a commitment to create a better future for yourself and those around you. These intrinsic motivations are often the most enduring, as they tap into the core of who you are and what you value.

Entrepreneurship can also be driven by the pursuit of impact. For some, the most fulfilling aspect of building a business is the ability to leave a positive mark on the world. Whether it's creating jobs, supporting underserved communities, or championing sustainability, the desire to contribute to something larger than yourself can be a powerful motivator. Individuals with this mindset often view their businesses not just as profit-generating entities but as vehicles for change. This perspective can provide an enduring sense of fulfillment, as the success of the business is measured not only in revenue but in the difference it makes.

While motivations vary widely, one common thread among successful entrepreneurs is clarity. It is not enough to feel vaguely inspired or vaguely dissatisfied with the status quo. To harness your drive effectively, you must articulate it clearly. This process involves introspection and honesty. It requires asking yourself tough questions and sitting with the answers, even when they reveal vulnerabilities or uncertainties. What is it that truly excites you? What are you willing to sacrifice for? What keeps you up at night, not with anxiety, but with anticipation? Answering these questions allows you to connect with your motivations on a deeper level, creating a foundation upon which you can build with confidence and resilience.

It's also important to recognize that motivations are not static. They evolve as you grow, as your business develops, and as the world around you changes. What drives you today may look different a year from now or ten years down the line. This is not a sign of inconsistency but of growth. The ability to adapt and realign your motivations is a critical skill in entrepreneurship. It ensures that your drive remains authentic and aligns with your current goals and circumstances. Periodically reflecting on your motivations can help you stay grounded and focused, even amid the whirlwind of running a business.

One of the most rewarding aspects of understanding your motivations is the way it connects you to others. When you are clear about what drives you, it becomes easier to communicate your vision to potential partners, investors, employees, and customers. People are naturally drawn to passion and purpose. They want to align themselves with leaders who have a clear sense of direction and who genuinely believe in what they are building. Your motivation can be a powerful tool for inspiring and rallying others to your cause.

At the same time, it is important to be wary of external pressures and expectations. Society often glorifies certain types of business motivations such as wealth, fame, and status while undervaluing others, such as creativity, community impact, or personal growth. While there is nothing wrong with aspiring to financial success, it is crucial to ensure that your motivations are your own and not dictated by societal norms or comparisons to others. Authenticity is key to sustainable success. When your drive comes from within, it is far more likely to endure the inevitable ups and downs of the journey.

In discovering your personal motivation, you are not only preparing yourself for the challenges of entrepreneurship but also setting the stage for a meaningful and fulfilling journey. The clearer you are about what drives you, the more effectively you can navigate the complex landscape of building and running a business. This clarity will serve as your compass, guiding your decisions, energizing your efforts, and reminding you why you started in the first place.

As you embark on this path, take the time to reflect deeply on your "why." Write it down, revisit it often, and let it evolve with you. Your motivation is the heartbeat of your entrepreneurial journey, the force that will sustain you through every challenge and celebrate with you in every success. When you truly understand what drives you, you are not only preparing to succeed but you are preparing to thrive.

Entrepreneurship is often seen as a pursuit of innovation and profit, but at its core, the most impactful ventures are those rooted in purpose. Purpose goes beyond the surface-level goal of making money; it speaks to the deeper reasons behind why you do what you do. It is the guiding principle that shapes your vision, decisions, and actions. Purpose gives your business meaning, connects you to your customers, and sustains you through challenges. When you build a business with a clear purpose, you create not just a livelihood but a legacy.

Purpose is the force that transforms a business idea from a simple transaction into a meaningful endeavor. When you have a clear purpose, your business becomes about more than just selling a product or service rather it becomes about creating value in the world. Value can take many forms: improving lives, solving problems, fostering community, or driving progress. This sense of meaning resonates deeply, both with you as the entrepreneur and with those who interact with your business. Customers are increasingly drawn to businesses that stand for something that align with their values and make them feel part of something bigger than themselves.

At the heart of purpose-driven entrepreneurship is the recognition that every business has the potential to make a difference. Whether you are running a small local operation or a global corporation, your business has an impact on your employees, your customers, your community, and the environment. The question is not whether your business will have an impact, but what kind of impact you want it to have. The purpose is the lens through which you define that impact. It is the intentional choice to align your business practices with your values and aspirations.

Defining your purpose begins with asking yourself what you care about most. What drives you to get out of bed in the morning? What problems in the world do you feel compelled to solve? What legacy do you want to leave behind? These questions can help you uncover the deeper motivations that fuel your spirit. Your purpose should be authentic, deeply personal, and aligned with your values. It is not about following trends or copying what others are doing; it is about staying true to who you are and what you believe in. For example, consider an entrepreneur who starts a sustainable fashion brand. Their purpose might be to combat the environmental damage caused by fast fashion by creating eco-friendly alternatives. This purpose shapes every aspect of their business, from the materials they use to their marketing strategy to the partnerships they form. It also resonates with customers who share the same values, creating a loyal community of supporters who believe in the brand's mission. This is the power of purpose: it not only guides the founder but also inspires others to join them on their journey.

It also acts as a powerful motivator during difficult times. Entrepreneurship is rarely a smooth ride; it is filled with obstacles, setbacks, and uncertainties. When the going gets tough, purpose becomes your anchor. It reminds you why you started in the first place and gives you the strength to keep going. It provides a sense of clarity and direction, helping you navigate challenges with resilience and determination. Entrepreneurs who are driven by purpose are less likely to give up when faced with adversity because they are deeply connected to the meaning behind their work.

Moreover, a strong sense of purpose can attract the right people to your business. This includes not only customers but also employees, partners, and investors. People want to be part of something meaningful. They want to work for companies that align with their values and make them feel proud of their contributions. They want to invest in ventures that are making a positive impact. When you have a clear and compelling purpose, you naturally attract like-minded individuals who share your vision and are willing to support you in achieving it.

It is also worth noting that purpose is not static. It can evolve as you and your business grow. What starts as a simple idea can develop into a larger mission as you gain experience, learn from your customers, and deepen your understanding of the impact you want to make. For example, an entrepreneur who initially started a food delivery service to make healthy meals accessible might later expand their purpose to include reducing food waste or supporting local farmers. This evolution is a natural part of the entrepreneurial journey and reflects the dynamic nature of purpose.

One of the key challenges in building a purpose-driven business is ensuring that your actions align with your stated purpose. It is not enough to simply declare your purpose; you must live it every day through your decisions and practices. This requires consistency, transparency, and accountability. Customers and stakeholders are quick to notice when a business's actions do not match its words. Authenticity is crucial to building trust and credibility. A purpose that is genuinely embedded in your business operations will resonate far more than one that exists only as a marketing slogan. Let's consider a tech company that claims to prioritize user privacy as part of its purpose. To live up to this claim, the company must make deliberate choices, such as investing in robust security measures, being transparent about data usage, and resisting practices that compromise user trust. These actions demonstrate a genuine commitment to the stated purpose and build a reputation for integrity. Purpose is not just about what you say, it is about what you do and how you do it.

The benefits of building a purpose-driven business extend beyond financial success. While profitability is important, this approach adds an extra layer of fulfillment to your business journey. It gives you a sense of pride and satisfaction that comes from knowing your work is making a difference. It connects you to something greater than yourself and helps you find meaning in the challenges and triumphs of entrepreneurship. Purpose allows you to measure success not just in terms of revenue but also in terms of impact. In building a business with purpose, you are not only creating value for yourself but also contributing to a larger ecosystem. Your purpose has the potential to inspire others, spark change, and drive progress. It is a powerful force that can turn a simple idea into a movement, a small business into a transformative enterprise. When you align your actions with your purpose, you create a ripple effect that extends far beyond the boundaries of your business.

It is also necessary to note that this industry is often romanticized as a pursuit fueled purely by passion. The narrative of "follow your passion" is inspiring and uplifting, but it is only part of the equation. While passion is a powerful motivator, it must be paired with practicality to create a sustainable and successful business. Passion gives you the energy to dream big, while practicality grounds those dreams in reality. Striking the balance between these two forces is essential for navigating the complexities of building a business.

Passion is the spark that ignites entrepreneurial ambition. It is the excitement you feel when you talk about your idea, the determination that keeps you up late working on a plan, and the hope that fuels your belief in a brighter future. It is deeply personal, rooted in your interests, values, and experiences. It connects you to your work in a way that is deeply fulfilling. It drives you to take risks, push boundaries, and innovate. Without passion, it is difficult to muster the perseverance needed to weather the inevitable challenges of entrepreneurship.

However, passion alone is not enough. Passion, untampered by practicality, can lead to unrealistic expectations, poor decision-making and unsustainable business practices. Entrepreneurs who rely solely on passion may find themselves pursuing ideas without properly assessing their feasibility or market potential. This can result in wasted resources, burnout, and disappointment. It must be channeled through the lens of practicality to create a business that is not only inspiring but also viable. Practicality involves approaching your business idea with a critical eye. It means conducting thorough research, understanding your target market, analyzing competitors, and evaluating the resources needed to bring your idea to life. Practicality requires you to ask tough questions: Is there a demand for your product or service? Can you deliver it profitably? What are the risks involved, and how will you mitigate them? While these questions may seem daunting, they are essential for ensuring that your passion translates into a business that can thrive.

The balance between passion and practicality begins with self-awareness. As an entrepreneur, you must understand your own strengths, weaknesses, and motivations. What are you truly passionate about, and why? What skills and knowledge do you bring to the table? Where do you need help? Being honest with yourself about these aspects allows you to leverage your passion effectively while addressing any gaps in your approach. Self-awareness also helps you stay focused on your goals and avoid being swayed by fleeting trends or external pressures.

One of the keyways to balance passion and practicality is by aligning your personal interests with market needs. Passion should not exist in a vacuum; it must intersect with a real-world problem that your business can solve. For example, if you are passionate about fitness, you might consider starting a business that addresses specific pain points in the fitness industry, such as affordable equipment, virtual coaching, or sustainable activewear. By aligning your passion with a genuine need, you create a business that is both meaningful to you and valuable to others.

Market research plays a crucial role in this process. Understanding your audience's needs, preferences, and behaviors allows you to refine your idea and ensure it resonates with potential customers. Research helps you identify gaps in the market, validate your assumptions, and tailor your offerings to meet demand. While passion may inspire your initial idea, research ensures that your idea is grounded in reality. It transforms your passion into a product or service that people are willing to pay for.

Another important aspect of balancing both concepts is setting realistic goals. Passion can sometimes lead entrepreneurs to set overly ambitious goals that are difficult to achieve. While it is important to dream big, those dreams must be broken down into actionable steps. Start small, test your ideas, and learn from the results. This iterative approach allows you to make adjustments and build momentum over time. Setting achievable milestones not only keeps you motivated but also reduces the risk of becoming overwhelmed.

Financial planning is another area where practicality is essential. Passionate entrepreneurs often underestimate the costs involved in starting and running a business. They may overlook expenses such as marketing, operations, and unforeseen challenges. Developing a detailed financial plan helps you understand the resources you need, manage cash flow, and avoid unnecessary risks. This does not mean that you need to stifle your creativity or ambition, it simply means that you need to be mindful of your financial realities and plan accordingly. Collaboration can also help you achieve this balance. Surrounding yourself with a team or network that complements your strengths allows you to harness both passion and practicality.

While practicality is important, it should not overshadow your passion. It is easy to become so focused on numbers and logistics that you lose sight of why you started your business in the first place. This can lead to a sense of disconnection and burnout. To maintain balance, it is important to regularly reconnect with your passion. Remind yourself of the bigger picture and the impact you want to create. Celebrate your achievements, no matter how small, and take time to reflect on your journey. Passion is what makes the hard work worth it, so don't let it fade. The balance between passion and practicality also extends to how you approach decision-making. Passion may lead you to pursue certain opportunities, but practicality ensures that you evaluate those opportunities carefully. For example, you might be excited about launching a new product, but practicality would require you to consider factors such as production costs, market demand, and timing. By weighing your decisions against both your passion and practical considerations, you can make choices that are both inspired and strategic.

It is also worth noting that passion and practicality are not opposing forces, they are complementary. Passion provides the energy and creativity needed to innovate, while practicality provides the structure and discipline needed to execute. Together, they create a dynamic balance that drives sustainable success. Think of passion as the fuel and practicality as the engine. Without fuel, the engine cannot run; without an engine, the fuel has no direction. Both are essential for the journey.

In today's entrepreneurial landscape, balancing passion and practicality is more important than ever. Customers are drawn to businesses that are authentic and purpose-driven, but they also expect professionalism and reliability. Investors look for founders who are passionate about their ideas but also capable of managing risks and delivering results. Balancing these expectations requires a mindset that embraces both creativity and pragmatism. Ultimately, the balance between passion and practicality is about staying true to yourself while adapting to the realities of the business world. It is about pursuing your dreams with intention and discipline. It is about finding joy in the process while staying focused on your goals. When you strike this balance, you create a business that is not only successful but also deeply fulfilling.

Navigating Risk and Resilience in Entrepreneurship.

This path is often described as a journey into the unknown, a path where certainty is scarce, and the potential for setbacks is high. A fundamental component is risk which is a concept that every entrepreneur must confront and embrace. Risk is not merely an inevitable part of starting a business; it is an essential ingredient in achieving success. How you navigate risk, manage uncertainty, and build resilience defines not only your entrepreneurial outcomes but also your personal growth.

Risk in entrepreneurship comes in many forms. It might be financial, where you invest personal savings or take on debt to fund your idea. It could be reputational, as you stake your credibility on a product or service that has yet to prove itself. There's also market risk, where customer demand might not meet your expectations, and operational risk, where unforeseen challenges disrupt your processes. Despite its intimidating nature, risk is not inherently negative. It represents opportunity and the chance to break new ground, solve problems, and create value.

The first step in navigating risk is to reframe your perception of it. Many people view risk as something to be avoided, a dangerous gamble that could lead to failure. However, seasoned entrepreneurs understand that risk is a necessary part of progress. Without risk, there is no reward. By embracing risk as a catalyst for growth, you can approach it with a mindset of curiosity and courage rather than fear and hesitation. It is best managed through preparation. While you cannot eliminate all uncertainty, you can equip yourself with the tools and knowledge to make informed decisions. Research is a powerful ally in this process. By understanding your market, competitors, and industry trends, you reduce the unknowns and gain clarity on potential challenges and opportunities. This due diligence forms the foundation of your risk management strategy, enabling you to anticipate obstacles and develop contingency plans.

Another effective way to manage it is by starting small and testing your ideas. Rather than diving headfirst into an unproven concept, consider launching a pilot program, creating a prototype, or conducting a limited release. These initial steps allow you to gather feedback, refine your approach, and address weaknesses before scaling up. This iterative process minimizes the stakes while maximizing your learning, giving you the confidence to move forward with greater certainty. A critical aspect of risk management is financial planning. Entrepreneurship often involves investing significant resources, and managing those resources wisely is key to mitigating risk. This begins with creating a detailed budget that accounts for both fixed and variable costs, as well as a realistic projection of revenue.

It also includes building a financial cushion which is a reserve of funds that can sustain you during lean periods or unexpected setbacks. While passion may drive your vision, a strong grasp of financial realities ensures its viability.

The ability to assess and prioritize risks is a skill that develops over time. Not all risks are created equally, and understanding which ones warrant your attention is crucial. Some risks, like launching a new product or entering a new market, have the potential for high rewards but also come with significant uncertainty. Others, such as refining an existing process, may carry lower stakes but can still impact your bottom line. By evaluating the likelihood and potential impact of each risk, you can allocate your resources and focus effectively.

While preparation and planning are vital, no amount of foresight can prevent every challenge. This is where resilience comes into play. Resilience is the capacity to recover quickly from setbacks and adapt to changing circumstances. It is a mindset that views failure not as a defeat but as a learning opportunity. In the entrepreneurial world, resilience is as important as innovation or strategy, as it enables you to keep moving forward despite adversity.

Resilience begins with self-awareness. Understanding your own emotional responses to stress, uncertainty, and failure helps you navigate difficult moments with clarity and composure. Developing emotional intelligence, which includes the ability to recognize and manage your emotions, empowers you to stay focused and make rational decisions under pressure. It also helps you maintain a positive outlook, even when faced with significant challenges. Building a support network is another cornerstone of resilience. Entrepreneurship can be a lonely journey, but surrounding yourself with mentors, peers, and advisors provides both practical guidance and emotional support. These connections offer valuable perspectives, help you troubleshoot problems, and remind you that you are not alone in your struggles. Sharing your experiences with others who have walked a similar path can be incredibly validating and inspiring.

Adaptability is a hallmark of resilient entrepreneurs. The business landscape is constantly evolving, and the ability to pivot in response to new information or changing conditions is essential. This might mean adjusting your product to better meet customer needs, exploring alternative revenue streams, or rethinking your marketing strategy. Adaptability requires a willingness to let go of preconceived notions and embrace change as an opportunity for growth.

Resilient entrepreneurs also understand the importance of maintaining their well-being. Burnout is a real risk in the fast-paced world of entrepreneurship, where long hours and high stakes are common. Taking care of your physical and mental health is not a luxury rather it is a necessity. This includes getting adequate sleep, eating well, exercising, and making time for hobbies and relationships outside of work. When you prioritize your well-being, you enhance your ability to think clearly, solve problems, and stay energized. The relationship between risk and resilience is a dynamic one. Taking risks inherently involves the possibility of setbacks, but it is resilience that allows you to bounce back and learn from those experiences. Every failure, misstep, or unexpected challenge is an opportunity to grow stronger and wiser. Over time, this cycle of risk-taking and recovery builds confidence, sharpening your instincts and expanding your capacity to handle uncertainty.

One of the most powerful tools for navigating risk and building resilience is a clear sense of purpose. When you are deeply connected to the "why" behind your business, you are better equipped to face challenges with determination and perspective. Purpose acts as your anchor during turbulent times, reminding you of the bigger picture and motivating you to persevere. It helps you stay focused on your goals and maintain a sense of meaning in your work, even when the journey feels difficult.

Another strategy for managing risk is diversification. Relying too heavily on a single product, market, or customer base increases your vulnerability to unforeseen disruptions. Diversification involves exploring multiple revenue streams, expanding your target audience, or developing complementary offerings. By spreading your risks, you reduce the impact of any single setback and create a more stable foundation for your business. Learning is at the heart of navigating risk and resilience. Every experience, whether successful or not, offers valuable insights that can inform your future decisions. Cultivating a growth mindset which is a belief in your ability to learn and improve empowers you to approach challenges with curiosity and openness. It encourages you to seek feedback, experiment with new ideas, and view failure as a steppingstone to success.

Technology can also play a role in risk management and resilience. Tools such as data analytics, project management software, and customer relationship management systems provide valuable insights and streamline operations, helping you make informed decisions and adapt to changing conditions. Embracing technology not only enhances efficiency but also positions your business to stay competitive in a rapidly evolving marketplace. Risk and resilience are inseparable elements of the entrepreneurial journey. Risk is the gateway to opportunity, while resilience is the strength that carries you through challenges. By approaching risk with preparation, curiosity, and a clear sense of purpose, you can navigate uncertainty with confidence. By cultivating resilience through self-awareness, adaptability, and support, you can overcome setbacks and emerge stronger. Together, these qualities form the foundation of success, enabling you to pursue your vision with courage, determination, and grace.

CHAPTER TWO
FROM IDEA TO EXECUTION

Opportunity is the cornerstone of entrepreneurship. It represents the gap between what is and what could be and a chance to create value, solve problems, and make an impact. But what exactly is an opportunity, and how does one recognize it? This question has puzzled and inspired individuals for generations. The nature of opportunity is complex, multifaceted, and deeply tied to the entrepreneurial mindset. To understand it fully, one must go beyond surface-level definitions and delve into the nuances that separate fleeting ideas from true opportunities.

An opportunity is a possibility that aligns with a need, a problem, or a desire in the market. It is the realization that a specific challenge exists and that you have the capability or resources to address it. Opportunities are not static; they are shaped by context, timing, and perspective. What appears to be a brilliant opportunity for one entrepreneur may go unnoticed by another. This subjectivity is a critical aspect of the journey, as it underscores the importance of individual insight and creativity.

A defining characteristic of opportunity is its inherent connection to change. Opportunities often arise from shifts in the environment whether economic, social, technological, or cultural. These changes create gaps or imbalances that present possibilities for innovation. For instance, the rise of digital communication and remote work in recent years has created opportunities for businesses offering virtual collaboration tools, online learning platforms, and remote workforce management solutions. Entrepreneurs who are attuned to such shifts are better positioned to identify and act on emerging trends. Opportunity is also closely linked to problems. At first glance, problems may seem like barriers or challenges to be avoided, but to the entrepreneur, they are fertile ground for ideas. The ability to recognize problems as potential opportunities is a hallmark of successful entrepreneurship. Problems reveal unmet needs, inefficiencies, or pain points that can be addressed through creative solutions.

However, not every problem is an opportunity, and not every opportunity is worth pursuing. The ability to discern between fleeting possibilities and meaningful opportunities requires critical thinking and analysis. A good opportunity is characterized by three key factors: feasibility, desirability, and viability. Feasibility refers to whether the opportunity can be implemented given the available resources, skills, and technology. Desirability reflects the extent to which the opportunity addresses a genuine need or demand. Viability, on the other hand, examines the long-term potential for profitability and sustainability.

Another crucial aspect of opportunity is its relationship to timing. Timing can make or break a venture. Being too early to market can result in low adoption rates, as seen with early Smartphone prototypes that preceded the infrastructure and consumer readiness for such technology. Conversely, entering the market too late means facing intense competition and limited differentiation. The right timing strikes a balance, allowing the entrepreneur to capitalize on readiness while staying ahead of competitors.

Opportunities can be categorized into two broad types: ordinary and transformative. Ordinary opportunities involve incremental improvements to existing products, services, or processes. These opportunities are often easier to identify and act upon, as they build on established foundations. For instance, adding new features to a popular software application or creating a localized version of a global product falls into this category. While these opportunities may not be out of the world, they can lead to steady growth and customer satisfaction.

Transformative opportunities, on the other hand, are game changers. They involve creating entirely new markets, redefining industries, or solving complex problems in innovative ways. Transformative opportunities are rarer and require a higher level of creativity, vision, and risk tolerance. Companies like Tesla and Airbnb exemplify the pursuit of transformative opportunities, as they challenged conventional norms and introduced disruptive solutions that reshaped their respective industries. While transformative opportunities hold immense potential, they also come with greater uncertainty and require a deep commitment to execution.

The process of recognizing opportunity begins with observation. Persons who are keen observers of their surroundings are better equipped to notice patterns, anomalies, and trends that others might overlook. Observation extends beyond the surface; it involves actively listening to customers, paying attention to emerging technologies, and staying informed about industry developments. This heightened awareness allows individuals to connect dots and uncover possibilities that lie hidden in plain sight. Creativity is another essential element in understanding the nature of opportunity. Creativity enables entrepreneurs to reimagine existing problems and solutions from new perspectives. It allows them to think beyond conventional boundaries and explore possibilities that others might deem impossible. It is not confined to artistic endeavors, but it is a skill that can be cultivated through practice, curiosity, and experimentation. By challenging assumptions and asking, "what if?" questions, persons unlock their potential to identify unique and valuable opportunities.

While observation and creativity are vital, they must be complemented by action. Opportunities are perishable; they have a limited window of relevance and potential. An idea left unexplored remains just that, an idea. Entrepreneurs must move beyond ideation to validation, testing their assumptions and gauging the feasibility of their concepts. This transition from recognition to execution is where opportunities are transformed into tangible outcomes.

It is also important to recognize that opportunities are not always obvious or handed to you on a silver platter. Many of the most successful entrepreneurial ventures were born out of adversity, frustration, or unmet needs that the founders experienced firsthand. Another dimension of opportunity is its relationship to risk. Opportunity and risk are two sides of the same coin. The greater the opportunity, the higher the likelihood of encountering challenges and uncertainties. This dynamic requires entrepreneurs to develop a balanced perspective which is embracing risk as an integral part of the journey while taking calculated steps to mitigate it. Opportunity also thrives on collaboration. No person operates in isolation, and opportunities are often discovered through interactions with others. Engaging with diverse perspectives, building networks, and seeking mentorship create fertile ground for idea generation and refinement. It also fosters partnerships and alliances that can amplify the impact of a venture.

Lastly, they are shaped by values and purpose. An opportunity that aligns with an entrepreneur's personal beliefs, values, and mission holds a deeper sense of meaning and motivation. When an entrepreneur's work resonates with their core identity, it becomes more than just a business and includes a source of fulfillment and impact. Purpose-driven opportunities not only benefit the entrepreneur but also create lasting value for customers, communities, and society as a whole.

Opportunities are born out of change, shaped by problems, and brought to life through entrepreneurial insight. They exist at the intersection of feasibility, desirability, and viability, and their success often depends on timing, collaboration, and alignment with purpose. By cultivating the ability to recognize and seize opportunities, entrepreneurs unlock their potential to create meaningful and lasting impact in the world. The journey to understanding opportunity is as much about perspective as it is about strategy, and it is a journey that defines the essence of entrepreneurship.

A vital question to ask is how I develop a mindset that not only sees these opportunities but be ready to take charge of them at all times. An entrepreneur's most valuable asset is not their capital, network, or even their outstanding idea, but it's their mindset. Specifically, it is a mindset primed to recognize, assess, and capitalize on opportunities, even in the most unlikely circumstances. Developing an opportunity-ready mindset is not just about being optimistic or ambitious; it is a deliberate practice of cultivating awareness, curiosity, and adaptability. This mindset enables persons to see potential where others see problems, to remain proactive amid uncertainty, and to take decisive action when others hesitate.

At the heart of an opportunity-ready mindset is the ability to perceive potential in everyday situations. Opportunities are rarely packaged neatly and presented on a silver platter. Instead, they are often disguised as challenges, inefficiencies, or gaps in the market. To see them requires a refined lens, a way of thinking that seeks to uncover hidden possibilities. This perspective is not innate; it is developed through deliberate effort and practice. It involves training the mind to move beyond the obvious question assumptions and explore alternative possibilities.

Curiosity is a cornerstone of this mindset. A curious entrepreneur approaches the world with an insatiable desire to learn and understand. They ask probing questions, investigate trends, and seek connections between seemingly unrelated ideas. Curiosity opens doors to discovery, as it encourages exploration and experimentation. Closely linked to curiosity is the willingness to challenge conventional thinking. The most successful entrepreneurs are those who refuse to accept the status quo. They view norms and traditions not as rigid rules but as starting points for innovation. By questioning why things are done a certain way, they uncover inefficiencies and imagine new approaches. Challenging the status quo is not about being contrarian for its own sake; it is about seeking improvement and pushing boundaries. This mindset fosters creativity and allows entrepreneurs to envision possibilities that others might overlook.

Adaptability is another critical trait of an opportunity-ready mindset. The business landscape is constantly shifting, shaped by technological advancements, changing consumer preferences, and global events. Entrepreneurs who cling rigidly to preconceived plans risk becoming obsolete. Conversely, those who embrace change and remain flexible can pivot their strategies to align with new realities. Self-awareness is equally vital in developing this mindset. Knowing one's strengths, weaknesses, and biases allows an entrepreneur to approach opportunities with clarity and realism. Self-awareness fosters humility, which is essential for seeking advice, collaborating with others, and recognizing when an idea requires refinement. It also helps entrepreneurs to manage emotions such as fear and overconfidence, ensuring that decisions are grounded in logic rather than impulsive reactions.

Another key ingredient is resilience. Entrepreneurs face countless obstacles on their journey, from financial struggles to market rejection. Without resilience, these challenges can become insurmountable barriers. However, with a resilient mindset, an entrepreneur views setbacks as valuable learning experiences. They analyze what went wrong, adjust their approach, and move forward with renewed determination. Resilience transforms failure from an endpoint into a steppingstone. The role of optimism cannot be understated. An optimistic entrepreneur sees possibilities where others see limitations. This does not mean ignoring risks or glossing over challenges; rather, it means maintaining a belief in one's ability to overcome obstacles and achieve success. Optimism fuels persistence, creativity, and enthusiasm, all of which are essential for identifying and pursuing opportunities. It also inspires confidence in others, whether they are investors, employees, or customers, creating a ripple effect that can amplify an entrepreneur's impact.

Another aspect of an opportunity-ready mindset is the ability to think in systems. Entrepreneurs who view the world as interconnected systems are better equipped to identify opportunities that exist within those systems. They understand how various components such as supply chains, consumer behaviors, and technological platforms interact and influence one another. These systems allows them to spot inefficiencies, anticipate ripple effects, and design solutions that create value across multiple touchpoints.

Time management and prioritization also play a significant role in this mindset. The most innovative individuals are not those who chase every idea but those who focus their energy on the most promising opportunities. Prioritization requires discernment and the ability to evaluate the potential impact, feasibility, and alignment of an opportunity with one's goals and values. By concentrating on what truly matters, entrepreneurs maximize their efforts and avoid spreading themselves too thin. Mentorship is another valuable resource for developing this mindset. A mentor provides guidance, shares experiences, and offers constructive feedback that helps refine your approach. Learning from someone who has navigated the entrepreneurial journey before you accelerates your growth and enhances your ability to recognize opportunities. Mentorship is not a one-way street; it is a relationship that encourages mutual learning and collaboration.

Reflection is a practice that strengthens the opportunity-ready mindset. Taking time to pause, evaluate, and synthesize experiences allows you to gain insights that might otherwise be missed. It helps you identify patterns, recognize areas for improvement, and celebrate successes. It also provides clarity on your values and long-term vision, ensuring that the opportunities you pursue align with your purpose.

Technology plays an increasingly significant role in shaping this mindset. Tools such as data analytics, artificial intelligence, and market research platforms provide entrepreneurs with valuable insights that inform decision-making. Technology enables you to track trends, measure impact, and forecast future scenarios with greater precision. Leveraging these tools enhances your ability to identify and act on opportunities in a timely and informed manner. Continuous learning cannot be overemphasized. The most successful entrepreneurs are lifelong learners who actively seek out knowledge and skills that enhance their capabilities. Whether through formal education, workshops, or self-directed study, continuous learning keeps you adaptable and informed. It also cultivates a growth-oriented mindset, which views challenges as opportunities to develop rather than as obstacles to avoid.

Finally, gratitude and mindfulness contribute to this mindset by grounding you in the present moment. Gratitude shifts your focus from what you lack to what you have, fostering a sense of abundance and possibility. Mindfulness, on the other hand, sharpens your awareness and helps you approach situations with clarity and intention. Together, these practices create a foundation of positivity and presence that enhances your ability to recognize and seize opportunities.

Tools and Frameworks for Identifying Opportunities.

Identifying these opportunities as earlier mentioned is an art and a science, a delicate blend of intuition and systematic analysis. While some individuals seem to possess an innate ability to spot potential where others see none, most successful entrepreneurs rely on tools and frameworks to refine their ability to discern opportunities. These tools are not merely instruments of analysis; they are enablers of insight, guiding persons in navigating complexity, uncovering hidden potential, and evaluating the viability of their ideas. Developing proficiency in these tools empowers entrepreneurs to turn raw observations into actionable opportunities.

The first and perhaps most intuitive tool is market research. Market research serves as the foundation for opportunity identification by providing a comprehensive understanding of consumer needs, preferences, and behaviors. It involves gathering and analyzing data from various sources, such as surveys, interviews, focus groups, and industry reports. Through market research, entrepreneurs can identify gaps in existing products or services, uncover unmet demands, and validate assumptions about potential customers.

A closely related framework is SWOT analysis, a structured approach to evaluating Strengths, Weaknesses, Opportunities, and Threats. Although commonly associated with strategic planning, SWOT analysis is equally valuable for opportunity identification. By assessing the external environment and internal capabilities, entrepreneurs can identify areas where they have a competitive advantage and where they might face challenges. For example, a business with strong technical expertise but limited market reach might identify an opportunity to partner with a distribution company to overcome its weakness. SWOT analysis encourages a holistic perspective, ensuring that opportunities are considered in the context of both internal potential and external factors.

Another indispensable tool is trend analysis, which involves studying patterns and developments in industries, markets, and consumer behavior over time. Trends provide valuable insights into where the world is heading and what opportunities may arise as a result. For instance, the widespread adoption of remote work during the COVID-19 pandemic sparked a surge in demand for tools that facilitate virtual collaboration, such as video conferencing software and project management platforms. Entrepreneurs who recognized this trend early were able to capitalize on the shift. Trend analysis requires not only observing current movements but also anticipating how they will evolve, enabling entrepreneurs to position themselves ahead of the curve.

In addition to examining external factors, entrepreneurs must also engage in problem identification. Every successful entrepreneurial venture begins with a problem that needs solving. Problems represent gaps between what exists and what is desired, creating opportunities for innovation. Tools such as the "Five Whys" technique, asking "why" repeatedly to uncover the root cause of an issue help individuals dig deeper into problems and understand their underlying drivers. Complementing problem identification is the use of design thinking, a human-centered approach to innovation. Design thinking emphasizes empathy, creativity, and iteration, focusing on understanding the needs and experiences of users. Entrepreneurs employing design thinking start by immersing themselves in the lives of their target audience, observing their behaviors and listening to their frustrations. They then brainstorm potential solutions, prototype their ideas, and test them with real users, refining the concepts based on feedback. This iterative process ensures that the opportunity pursued is both desirable to customers and feasible to implement.

Another framework that has gained prominence is the Business Model Canvas, a visual tool for mapping out the key components of a business idea. The canvas consists of nine building blocks, including value propositions, customer segments, revenue streams, and key resources. By filling out the canvas, entrepreneurs can systematically explore the viability of an opportunity and identify areas that require further validation. Opportunities often emerge from patterns and anomalies, making data analysis an invaluable tool. With the proliferation of data in today's digital world, entrepreneurs have access to a wealth of information about consumer behavior, market trends, and industry performance. Analytical tools such as Google Analytics, social media insights, and predictive modeling enable entrepreneurs to identify emerging patterns that signal opportunities. Data analysis enhances decision-making by providing evidence-based insights that reduce uncertainty.

Entrepreneurs can also benefit from scenario planning, a strategic framework for envisioning multiple potential futures. Scenario planning involves identifying key drivers of change, such as technological advancements or regulatory shifts, and exploring how these drivers might interact to create different scenarios. By imagining a range of possibilities, entrepreneurs can identify opportunities that are resilient across various outcomes. Crowdsourcing is another innovative approach to identifying opportunities. By engaging with a diverse group of people, entrepreneurs can tap into collective intelligence and uncover insights that might otherwise remain hidden. It can take many forms, from hosting online idea competitions to gathering feedback through social media polls. This approach not only generates ideas but also builds a sense of community and engagement around the entrepreneurial venture.

In addition to leveraging tools and frameworks, entrepreneurs must cultivate the habit of active listening. Listening to customers, employees, industry experts, and even competitors provides a wealth of information about potential opportunities. For instance, customer complaints often highlight pain points that can be transformed into innovative solutions. An entrepreneur who listens attentively to feedback about a cumbersome checkout process might develop a streamlined payment system that enhances the customer experience. Active listening goes beyond hearing words; it involves understanding emotions, motivations, and unmet needs, creating a foundation for meaningful opportunity identification.

Opportunities also arise from benchmarking, a process of comparing one's business or idea to industry standards and best practices. Benchmarking reveals gaps in performance, highlighting areas for improvement and innovation. It is not about copying competitors; it is about learning from their successes and failures to create a unique and competitive offering.

Networking plays a pivotal role in opportunity identification. Building relationships with peers, mentors, investors, and industry professionals expands an entrepreneur's perspective and exposes them to new ideas. Networking events, industry conferences, and online communities provide platforms for exchanging knowledge and discovering emerging trends. Moreover, networking fosters collaboration, enabling entrepreneurs to partner with others who have complementary skills and resources. These connections often lead to serendipitous discoveries that spark innovative opportunities.

The practice of questioning assumptions is also vital. Many potential opportunities go unnoticed because they lie beneath layers of accepted practices and norms. Challenging the status quo allows entrepreneurs to uncover inefficiencies or problems hidden in plain sight. Consider the evolution of transportation services. For decades, people relied on traditional taxi services without questioning their limitations until companies like Uber and Lyft reimagined the system. These entrepreneurs saw the inefficiencies in hailing cabs, pricing structures, and service availability as opportunities to innovate. By questioning what most took for granted, they created an entirely new industry.

Perspective matters greatly when seeking opportunities in unlikely places. Often, the way you frame a situation determines whether you see possibilities or dismiss them entirely. Individuals who adopt a positive, solutions-oriented perspective tend to find opportunities even in adversity. Another crucial factor is the ability to look beyond immediate appearances. Many opportunities are cloaked in layers of complexity or disguised as unappealing challenges. An unpolished idea, a disorganized market, or a seemingly small niche can often yield tremendous value with the right approach. It also involves connecting the dots between seemingly unrelated ideas or trends. This requires lateral thinking which is the ability to draw insights and parallels from diverse domains. The key is to view the world as an interconnected system, where ideas and industries overlap in unexpected ways.

Empathy plays a powerful role in spotting possibilities that others might miss. Entrepreneurs who take the time to understand the needs and struggles of others often discover ways to create meaningful solutions. Empathy enables you to put yourself in someone else's shoes, whether it's a busy parent trying to juggle responsibilities, a small business owner grappling with cash flow issues, or a student facing barriers to education. By identifying with their experiences, you can uncover opportunities to improve their lives in ways that resonate deeply. Cultural and geographical differences also hold untapped potential for entrepreneurs willing to look beyond their familiar environments. Traveling to new places or studying the practices of different cultures can provide fresh perspectives and reveal opportunities to adapt successful ideas from one context to another.

Recognizing opportunities also requires trusting your instincts while also relying on informed analysis. Sometimes, an idea or a situation might not fit neatly into existing frameworks, but it sparks a sense of potential that's hard to ignore. Balancing intuition with critical thinking enables entrepreneurs to pursue ideas that others might overlook.

Opportunities are everywhere, even in the most unexpected corners of the world. To uncover them, entrepreneurs must cultivate curiosity, challenge assumptions, and adopt diverse perspectives. They must be empathetic, persistent, and willing to learn from failure, using creativity and innovation to transform challenges into possibilities. By exploring intersections, leveraging technology, and collaborating with others, entrepreneurs can find value in overlooked spaces and redefine what is possible. Recognizing opportunities in unlikely places is not just about seeing what others miss; it is about having the courage and vision to turn the unthinkable into reality.

CHAPTER THREE
THE ENTREPRENEURIAL MINDSET: THINKING BIG, STARTING SMALL

Building a business is an exciting journey, but it is also fraught with challenges, and one of the most significant hurdles entrepreneurs faces is navigating financial constraints. For those venturing into entrepreneurship, the question of how to manage limited resources and secure the necessary capital often looms large. Without adequate funding, even the most promising ideas can wither before they have the chance to thrive. Overcoming these challenges requires strategic thinking, creative problem-solving, and a relentless commitment to making the most of what is available.

Managing financial constraints is the ability to maximize existing resources. Entrepreneurs often find themselves in situations where they must do more with less, stretching every penny to cover essential expenses while driving their business forward. This requires a mindset that prioritizes efficiency and ingenuity. For instance, rather than investing in expensive office spaces, many startups operate remotely or use co-working spaces to save costs. Similarly, instead of hiring a full team of employees in the early stages, entrepreneurs can rely on contractors, freelancers, or part-time help to handle specific tasks. The key is to focus on spending money where it matters most such as on activities that directly contribute to growth and sustainability.

Another crucial strategy for navigating financial constraints is bootstrapping. Bootstrapping involves funding a business using personal savings, revenue generated by the business, or support from friends and family, without relying on external investors or loans. While this approach requires significant discipline and sacrifices, it also allows entrepreneurs to retain full control over their business. This approach forces entrepreneurs to be resourceful, helping them develop lean operations that can sustain the business through challenging times.

However, personal resources and bootstrapping alone are not always sufficient, especially when a business requires substantial capital to scale. In such cases, persons must look to external sources of funding. One of the most common options is seeking investments from venture capitalists (VCs) or angel investors. These individuals or firms provide funding in exchange for equity in the company, betting on the business's potential for growth and profitability. While securing investment from VCs or angel investors can be highly beneficial, it requires entrepreneurs to present a compelling case for their business. This includes developing a detailed business plan, demonstrating market demand, and showcasing a clear path to profitability. It is also essential to find investors whose values and vision align with those of the entrepreneur, as this partnership can significantly influence the direction of the business.

For entrepreneurs who prefer not to relinquish equity, business loans and grants offer an alternative path to funding. Banks and financial institutions provide loans to businesses with solid credit histories and strong business plans. Government programs and nonprofit organizations also offer grants to entrepreneurs, particularly those operating in specific industries or addressing social challenges. Unlike loans, grants do not need to be repaid, making them an attractive option for startups and small businesses. However, the application process for grants can be competitive and time-consuming, requiring entrepreneurs to demonstrate their impact and align with the grant's objectives.

Beyond these traditional methods, the rise of crowdfunding platforms has revolutionized the way entrepreneurs raise capital. Platforms like Kickstarter, Indiegogo, and GoFundMe allow entrepreneurs to pitch their ideas directly to the public and raise funds from a broad audience. It not only provides access to capital but also serves as a way to validate ideas and build a community of early supporters. The success of this method depends on the entrepreneur's ability to tell a compelling story, demonstrate the value of their product or service, and engage their audience effectively. While securing funding is crucial, managing the resources at hand is equally important. This involves creating and adhering to a realistic budget. A well-structured budget allows entrepreneurs to track income and expenses, identify areas where costs can be reduced, and allocate funds to priority areas. Budgeting is not a one-time activity but an ongoing process that requires regular review and adjustments based on changing circumstances. Individuals who master the art of budgeting gain greater control over their finances and can make informed decisions that drive the success of their business.

Another aspect of resource management is optimizing cash flow. Cash flow represents the movement of money in and out of a business, and maintaining a positive cash flow is critical for survival and growth. Entrepreneurs must ensure that their revenue streams are consistent and sufficient to cover operational expenses. This can be achieved by negotiating favorable payment terms with suppliers, incentivizing early payments from customers, and maintaining a cash reserve for emergencies. Tools like accounting software and financial dashboards can provide relevant insights into cash flow, helping founders stay on top of their finances.

Partnerships and collaborations can also play a significant role in overcoming financial constraints. By partnering with other businesses, entrepreneurs can share resources, reduce costs, and access new markets. Leveraging technology can help entrepreneurs manage financial constraints effectively. Digital tools and platforms enable businesses to automate processes, reduce manual effort, and improve efficiency. For example, customer relationship management (CRM) software can streamline sales and marketing activities, while cloud-based accounting software simplifies financial management. E-commerce platforms provide entrepreneurs with affordable ways to reach customers and sell products without the need for physical stores. By embracing technology, persons can achieve cost savings while enhancing their operational capabilities.

Despite these strategies, financial constraints often create significant stress and pressure for entrepreneurs. To navigate these challenges successfully, it is essential to cultivate a mindset of resilience and adaptability as earlier discussed. Resilience allows entrepreneurs to persevere in the face of setbacks, while adaptability enables them to pivot and explore alternative approaches when needed. Mentorship and networking can provide valuable support in navigating financial challenges. Experienced mentors can offer guidance on managing resources, securing funding, and making strategic decisions. Networking with other entrepreneurs can also lead to opportunities for collaboration, shared knowledge, and access to funding sources. These connections often prove invaluable, providing both practical assistance and emotional encouragement.

Building a successful business requires navigating a complex and often unforgiving market landscape. Entrepreneurs face relentless competition, shifting consumer demands, and the constant need to differentiate their offerings. These market and competition pressures are an inherent part of the entrepreneurial journey, and overcoming them demands a blend of strategy, innovation, and resilience. By understanding the dynamics of their industry, staying attuned to customer needs, and leveraging their unique strengths, entrepreneurs can not only survive but thrive in competitive markets.

One of the first steps in addressing market pressures is conducting a thorough market analysis. Understanding the industry in which you operate is critical to identifying opportunities and threats. Market analysis involves studying factors such as customer demographics, buying behaviors, market size, and emerging trends. This data allows entrepreneurs to identify gaps in the market that their products or services can fill. Second is conducting competitive research which is essential. Knowing who your competitors are, what they offer, and how they operate can provide valuable insights into your own business strategy. Competitive research involves examining competitors' pricing models, marketing tactics, customer reviews, and product features. This process helps entrepreneurs understand what their competitors are doing well and where they might be falling short.

However, knowing the competition is not enough; entrepreneurs must also find ways to differentiate their offerings. Differentiation is the cornerstone of standing out in a crowded market. This can be achieved by offering unique value propositions, features or benefits that set your product or service apart. The key is to focus on what makes your business distinctive and communicate that clearly to your audience.

Building a strong brand identity is another powerful way to tackle market and competition pressures. A compelling brand goes beyond logos and slogans; it encompasses the values, mission, and personality of a business. A well-defined brand resonates with customers, fosters loyalty, and creates an emotional connection that competitors cannot easily replicate. Consider companies like Apple, which have built brands synonymous with innovation and quality. Entrepreneurs can craft their brand identity by identifying their core values, understanding their target audience, and consistently delivering on their promises. In highly competitive markets, pricing strategies can play a decisive role in attracting and retaining customers. Pricing is not merely a matter of setting numbers; it is a strategic decision that reflects your business goals, target audience, and market positioning. For instance, premium pricing might appeal to customers who associate higher prices with quality and exclusivity, while competitive pricing can attract budget-conscious consumers. Dynamic pricing, where prices are adjusted based on demand and market conditions, can also be effective in certain industries. The challenge lies in striking a balance between profitability and customer appeal, ensuring that your pricing strategy aligns with your overall business objectives.

Adapting to changing market conditions is another critical skill for entrepreneurs. Markets are dynamic, influenced by factors such as technological advancements, economic shifts, and evolving consumer preferences. Businesses that fail to adapt risk becoming obsolete, while those that embrace change can seize new opportunities. A customer-centric approach is one of the most effective ways to address market pressures. Listening to and understanding your customers enables you to deliver products and services that meet their needs and expectations. Building strong relationships with customers through personalized communication and exceptional service fosters loyalty and encourages repeat business. Entrepreneurs who prioritize their customers often find that satisfied customers become advocates, helping to drive growth through word-of-mouth referrals and positive reviews.

Effective marketing and communication are vital tools for navigating competitive markets. Entrepreneurs must be able to convey the value of their offerings in a way that resonates with their target audience. This involves selecting the right channels, crafting compelling messages, and employing creative campaigns that capture attention. Digital marketing has become particularly important, offering businesses the ability to reach a global audience through social media, search engine optimization (SEO), and email marketing. By leveraging these tools, entrepreneurs can amplify their visibility and establish a strong presence in the market.

Forming alliances with complementary businesses allows for shared resources, expanded reach, and mutual support. Entrepreneurs must also be prepared to face external pressures, such as regulatory challenges and economic fluctuations. Regulations can vary widely depending on industry and location, creating barriers to entry or compliance costs. Entrepreneurs need to stay informed about relevant laws and regulations, seeking legal advice when necessary to navigate complex requirements. Economic downturns or unexpected events, such as pandemics, can also disrupt markets and force businesses to adapt quickly. During such times, maintaining financial discipline, diversifying revenue streams, and building contingency plans become crucial.

Innovation is a powerful antidote to competition. By fostering a culture of continuous improvement and creativity, persons can stay ahead of the curve and respond proactively to market demands. Innovation does not always mean inventing something entirely new; it can involve enhancing existing products, improving processes, or finding new ways to engage customers. Data-driven decision-making allows entrepreneurs to analyze trends, track performance, and identify opportunities for improvement. Technology also enables automation, reducing costs and increasing efficiency. By harnessing the power of data and technology, entrepreneurs can make informed decisions and stay ahead in a fast-paced market.

Operational and organizational hurdles are obstacles often encountered by individuals in running a smooth business operation. Behind every successful business lies a framework of operations and an organized team that ensures everything runs smoothly. However, building and maintaining this foundation is far from straightforward. Entrepreneurs frequently encounter challenges in establishing efficient processes, recruiting and retaining talent, and scaling operations to meet growing demands. Overcoming these operational and organizational hurdles requires a mix of strategic planning, adaptability, and strong leadership.

A pressing operational challenge faced is setting up effective workflows and systems. Early-stage businesses often operate in a chaotic environment, where tasks are handled on an ad hoc basis without clear procedures in place. While this approach might work temporarily, it quickly becomes unsustainable as the business grows. Entrepreneurs must invest time and effort into defining workflows that streamline tasks, reduce redundancies, and enhance productivity. Time management is another critical aspect of operational efficiency. Entrepreneurs often wear multiple hats, juggling responsibilities that range from product development to customer service. Without proper time management, tasks can pile up, deadlines can be missed, and the quality of work can suffer. Tools such as project management software, shared calendars, and task prioritization frameworks like the Eisenhower Matrix can help entrepreneurs stay organized and focused. Delegating responsibilities to capable team members is equally important, allowing leaders to focus on strategic decisions rather than getting bogged down in day-to-day operations.

As businesses grow, the complexity of operations increases and the need for scalable systems becomes apparent. Scaling operations involves expanding capacity to meet rising demand without compromising quality or efficiency. However, scaling is not just about adding resources; it also requires careful planning to avoid overextension. Entrepreneurs must analyze market trends, forecast demand, and assess their financial readiness before scaling their operations.

Recruiting and retaining talent pose significant organizational challenges, particularly for startups and small businesses that may not have the resources to offer competitive salaries or extensive benefits. However, attracting top talent is not solely monetary compensation. Individuals can differentiate their businesses by offering a compelling vision, opportunities for professional growth, and a positive work culture. Once talent is onboarded, the challenge shifts to building a cohesive and motivated team. Effective communication is the cornerstone of a strong team dynamic. Entrepreneurs must ensure that team members understand their roles, responsibilities, and how their work contributes to the broader goals of the organization. Regular meetings, clear communication channels, and an open-door policy can foster transparency and trust within the team. Additionally, recognizing and rewarding achievements helps to boost morale and create a sense of belonging among employees.

Leadership plays a crucial role in overcoming organizational hurdles. Entrepreneurs must embody the qualities of a strong leader: vision, empathy, decisiveness, and the ability to inspire others. Leadership is particularly important during times of change or uncertainty, such as when a company pivots its strategy or faces financial difficulties. In such moments, employees look to their leaders for guidance and reassurance. By communicating openly, addressing concerns, and demonstrating a commitment to shared goals, entrepreneurs can rally their teams and maintain a sense of unity.

Another common organizational challenge is managing conflicts within the team. Disagreements and misunderstandings are inevitable in any workplace, but how they are handled can make or break a team's cohesion. Founders must develop conflict resolution skills to address issues promptly and constructively. Encouraging open dialogue, promoting active listening, and finding solutions that address the concerns of all parties involved can help resolve conflicts and prevent them from escalating. Apart from internal challenges, entrepreneurs must also navigate external operational hurdles, such as supply chain disruptions, regulatory compliance, and market volatility. Supply chain issues, for instance, can lead to delays, increased costs, and customer dissatisfaction. Entrepreneurs must build resilient supply chains by diversifying suppliers, maintaining safety stock, and leveraging technology to improve visibility and coordination. Similarly, staying informed about industry regulations and ensuring compliance is essential to avoid legal penalties and maintain credibility with stakeholders.

Operational excellence also depends on the ability to measure and monitor performance. Key performance indicators (KPIs) provide valuable insights into how well a business is functioning and highlight areas for improvement. Regular performance reviews, feedback loops, and benchmarking against industry standards are essential practices for continuous improvement.

Entrepreneurs must also tackle the challenge of building and maintaining company culture. Culture is the invisible force that shapes how employees behave, interact, and approach their work. A positive culture fosters collaboration, innovation, and loyalty, while a toxic culture can lead to high turnover and low morale. Leaders must actively shape their company culture by defining core values, leading by example, and creating an environment where employees feel valued and empowered. Amid all these operational and organizational challenges, entrepreneurs must remain adaptable. The business environment is constantly evolving, and the ability to pivot is crucial for long-term success. Whether it's adopting new technologies, entering new markets, or reorganizing workflows, adaptability allows businesses to stay relevant and competitive. Persons who embrace change and view challenges as opportunities for growth are better equipped to navigate the complexities of running a business. Collaboration with external partners can also alleviate operational burdens. Outsourcing non-core activities such as payroll processing, IT support, or marketing allows entrepreneurs to focus on their core competencies.

Starting and scaling a business is often constrained by the reality of limited resources. Financial challenges, in particular, remain a defining hurdle for many entrepreneurs. Whether it's securing initial funding, managing cash flow, or allocating scarce resources, entrepreneurs must demonstrate both creativity and prudence to thrive. Navigating these constraints is not just about survival; it's about using limitations as a catalyst for innovation and strategic thinking.

As earlier discussed, an immediate challenge entrepreneur's face is raising capital to launch their business. While some may have personal savings or access to family loans, many must rely on external funding sources such as investors, bank loans, or crowdfunding. Each funding route comes with its own set of opportunities and challenges. For instance, securing investment from venture capitalists often means ceding some control of the business, while traditional bank loans require a solid credit history and the ability to repay debts promptly. Persons must weigh these options carefully, considering not only the financial implications but also the long-term impact on their business goals.

For many, the solution lies in bootstrapping which entails building a business with minimal external funding. Bootstrapping often requires a mindset of frugality and a willingness to prioritize essentials over luxuries. Entrepreneurs may need to rely on personal savings, seek out low-cost resources, or start small and reinvest profits to fuel growth. While this approach can be challenging, it fosters a sense of ownership and discipline, as every dollar spent is carefully scrutinized. Effective cash flow management is another cornerstone of navigating financial constraints. Even profitable businesses can fail if they run out of cash to cover operational expenses. Entrepreneurs must monitor their inflows and outflows carefully, ensuring that they have enough liquidity to meet short-term obligations while planning for long-term growth. They must also stay vigilant about identifying new opportunities for revenue generation. Diversifying income streams reduces dependence on a single source of revenue and provides a buffer against market fluctuations.

Persons must also optimize their use of non-financial resources. Time, talent, and physical assets are often in short supply, particularly in the early stages of a business. Entrepreneurs need to adopt a resourceful mindset, finding ways to do more with less. Strategic prioritization is pivotal to making the most of limited resources. Founders must identify their most critical goals and allocate resources accordingly. This often means saying no to opportunities that don't align with their vision or delaying certain projects until the necessary resources are available. For example, a tech startup might prioritize developing a minimum viable product (MVP) over building a full-featured platform, allowing it to test the market and gather feedback before committing to larger investments. While financial and resource constraints are challenging, they often drive innovation and creativity. Entrepreneurs operating within tight budgets are forced to think outside the box, finding unconventional solutions to problems.

Long-term planning is essential to overcome financial and resource constraints sustainably. Individuals must balance short-term needs with their long-term vision, making decisions that support growth without jeopardizing stability. This might involve setting clear financial goals, creating detailed budgets, and regularly reviewing progress. Despite these challenges, it's important to recognize that constraints can also serve as a filter for identifying the most committed and capable entrepreneurs. Those who persevere despite limited resources often emerge stronger, with a deeper understanding of their business and a more focused approach to growth. Constraints force entrepreneurs to prioritize, innovate, and build lean operations, qualities that are invaluable as the business grows and scales.

CHAPTER FOUR
CRAFTING YOUR BUSINESS PLAN

There is no entrepreneur without a business and no business without a business plan.

A business plan is more than just a formal document filled with financial forecasts and market analyses; it is the foundation of the execution of your ideas. Basically, it serves as a roadmap, guiding you from the initial spark of an idea to its execution and beyond. For aspiring entrepreneurs, understanding its purpose is crucial. This document is not merely an academic exercise; it is a strategic tool that provides clarity, attracts resources, and sets the stage for success. At its simplest, a business plan outlines the "what," "why," and "how" of your business idea. It defines what you want to achieve, why your venture is worth pursuing, and how you plan to bring it to life. Without this blueprint, it's easy to lose focus or misallocate resources, especially in the dynamic and often unpredictable world of entrepreneurship.

For the entrepreneur, the business plan is a tool of self-discovery. Writing it forces you to think critically about every aspect of your idea. What problem are you solving? Who are your customers? What resources do you need? What are the risks, and how will you mitigate them? These questions are not merely academic; they shape the foundation of your business. The clearer your answers, the stronger your foundation will be. Moreover, it is instrumental in aligning your vision with actionable steps. By translating abstract ideas into a structured framework, you can identify gaps, opportunities, and potential pitfalls. This exercise ensures that your excitement for the idea is matched by a practical understanding of its feasibility.

In the early stages of growing your endeavor, enthusiasm often outpaces clarity. The allure of pursuing multiple opportunities simultaneously can lead to scattered efforts and inefficiencies. A business plan counteracts this tendency by serving as a compass. It forces you to prioritize, focus on specific objectives, and allocate resources effectively. For instance, consider an entrepreneur who dreams of launching an eco-friendly clothing line. Without a business plan, their vision might include vague notions of sustainability and fashion trends. However, a structured plan compels them to address critical questions:

What materials will be used, and how will they be sourced?

Who is the target customer, and what are their preferences?

What is the pricing strategy, and how does it compare to competitors?

By answering these questions, the entrepreneur gains clarity, enabling them to refine their idea into a tangible business model.

One of the most critical roles of a business plan is its ability to attract resources. Whether you are seeking investment, partnerships, or loans, a well-crafted business plan is often the first impression stakeholders have of your venture. Investors, in particular, rely on business plans to assess the viability and potential profitability of a business. For this reason, your business plan must be clear, concise, and compelling. It should demonstrate a thorough understanding of the market, articulate a unique value proposition, and present realistic financial projections. A strong business plan reassures investors that you have done your homework and are prepared to manage the risks associated with your idea.

Beyond financial investors, business plans can also attract other resources, such as skilled team members or strategic partnerships. Potential collaborators are more likely to join your venture if they see a clear roadmap and believe in your vision. Similarly, suppliers and vendors may offer better terms if they perceive your business as stable and well-organized. Running a business involves countless decisions, from choosing suppliers to launching marketing campaigns. It provides a framework for making these decisions systematically and confidently. It helps you evaluate options based on how they align with your goals and overall strategy. For example, suppose your business plan emphasizes customer-centric innovation. When faced with a decision to cut costs by compromising product quality, you can refer back to your plan to evaluate whether this aligns with your core values and objectives. This structured approach ensures consistency and reduces the likelihood of impulsive or counterproductive decisions.

It's important to recognize that a business plan is not a one-size-fits-all document. Depending on your audience, you may need to tailor your plan to highlight different aspects. For instance, investors emphasize financial projections, market potential, and return on investment. For partners, focus on shared goals, collaboration opportunities, and long-term vision and for internal use, highlight operational details, milestones, and strategies for day-to-day execution. This adaptability ensures that your business plan remains relevant in various contexts while maintaining its core message.

A common misconception is that a business plan is a static document created once and forgotten. In reality, it is a living tool that evolves alongside your business. As market conditions change or new opportunities arise, your business plan should be updated to reflect these developments. Consider the example of a tech startup initially focused on developing a niche app for freelancers. Over time, they discover a broader market among small businesses. Updating their business plan to reflect this shift allows them to realign resources, revise marketing strategies, and pursue new growth opportunities. Finally, a business plan builds confidence not only in you as the entrepreneur but also in those who support your venture. The act of creating the plan demonstrates your commitment, discipline, and willingness to confront challenges head-on. For stakeholders, a robust business plan signals that you are prepared for the realities of entrepreneurship. It reassures them that their investment, whether financial or otherwise, is in capable hands. For you, the entrepreneur, the plan provides a sense of direction and control, reducing uncertainty and boosting your confidence to navigate the complexities of running a business.

Understanding the purpose of a business plan is the first step in building a strong foundation for your entrepreneurial journey. It is not just a document but is a tool for clarity, focus, and decision-making. It aligns your vision with actionable steps, attracts resources, and provides the confidence needed to turn your idea into a thriving business. This plan is only as effective as the components it includes. While the specific details may vary depending on the nature of your business, the fundamental elements remain consistent. Each component serves a distinct purpose, contributing to a cohesive narrative that not only outlines your vision but also demonstrates its feasibility. To craft a robust business plan, understanding these components and their roles is essential.

The first and perhaps most critical part of any business plan is the executive summary. Though brief, this section must capture the essence of your business. It serves as an introduction, offering readers a snapshot of your goals, your product or service, and your intended impact. For many investors or stakeholders, the executive summary may be the only part of your plan they read, making it crucial to convey the most compelling aspects of your business clearly and concisely. An effective executive summary leaves readers intrigued, eager to explore the details in the subsequent sections.

The next significant component is the market analysis. A well-researched market analysis demonstrates your understanding of the industry, your target audience, and the competitive landscape. This section requires more than a surface-level overview; it demands in-depth research and thoughtful insights. Understanding your market begins with identifying your target audience. Who are your ideal customers? What are their demographics, behaviors, and needs? This understanding is critical not only for developing your product or service but also for tailoring your marketing and sales strategies to reach them effectively. In addition to customer insights, your market analysis should address the competitive landscape. This involves identifying your competitors, analyzing their strengths and weaknesses, and determining your position within the market. The goal here is not to downplay competitors but to showcase your unique value proposition. What sets your business apart? Whether it's innovation, cost-efficiency, or superior customer service, your plan should articulate what makes your business distinct and how it will gain an edge in the market.

Closely tied to the market analysis is the marketing and sales strategy. This section outlines how you intend to attract and retain customers. It should delve into the specifics of your branding, pricing, distribution channels, and promotional efforts. Effective marketing is not just about reaching people; it's about creating a connection with your audience. This requires understanding their motivations and crafting messages that resonate with them. Your sales strategy, on the other hand, focuses on converting potential customers into actual buyers. Will you rely on direct sales, e-commerce, or partnerships? How will you handle customer service and support? These details give stakeholders confidence that you have a clear plan for generating revenue and building customer loyalty.

The operational plan is another critical component, providing a behind-the-scenes look at how your business will function. This section should detail your processes, from sourcing materials to delivering products or services to customers. It should also address logistical considerations, such as location, equipment, and staffing. The operational plan gives a sense of the day-to-day realities of running your business, ensuring that it is not only visionary but also grounded in practicality.

No business plan is complete without financial projections. This section transforms your vision into numbers, illustrating the financial viability of your business. Key elements include income statements, cash flow statements, and balance sheets, projected over a defined period, typically three to five years. While it's impossible to predict the future with absolute certainty, your financial projections should be based on realistic assumptions and data. Investors, in particular, will scrutinize this section to assess the potential return on their investment. Therefore, it's essential to be transparent and detailed. Break down your revenue streams, highlight key expenses, and outline your funding requirements. If you're seeking a loan or investment, specify how these funds will be used to drive growth or address challenges.

Many business plans also include supplemental sections tailored to the specific needs of the business. For instance, a technology startup may include a section on intellectual property and research and development. Similarly, a nonprofit organization might focus on its mission and social impact. These sections provide an opportunity to address unique aspects of your business that don't fit neatly into the standard framework.

Throughout your business plan, it's essential to maintain a cohesive narrative. Each component should be built on the others, creating a comprehensive and compelling story. Avoid treating sections as isolated silos; instead, weave them together to illustrate how every aspect of your business contributes to your overarching vision. For example, your marketing strategy should align with your target audience identified in the market analysis, while your operational plan should support the financial goals outlined in your projections. Another important consideration is the tone and style of your writing. Your business plan should strike a balance between professionalism and accessibility. Avoid overly technical jargon or dense language that might alienate readers unfamiliar with your industry. At the same time, ensure that your tone reflects your confidence and passion for your business. Clarity and precision are paramount. Each section should be concise yet thorough, avoiding unnecessary fluff or repetition. Use visuals, such as charts and graphs, to convey complex information more effectively. For instance, a well-designed chart can make your financial projections more digestible, while a graph illustrating market trends can reinforce your analysis.

It's also worth noting that while a business plan is a formal document, it should reflect your unique voice and perspective. This personal touch can make your plan more engaging and memorable. Stakeholders want to feel your enthusiasm and conviction; they want to believe not just in your business but also in you as its leader.

While the details of financial projections, marketing strategies, and operational logistics are essential, their purpose is to serve a larger narrative: the story of where you want your business to go and how you plan to get there. Aligning your business plan with your vision and goals is a critical step in creating a cohesive and actionable document that remains relevant throughout the lifecycle of your venture.

A vision represents the "why" behind your business. It is the foundation that supports every decision you make; from the products you develop to the markets you serve. Without a clear vision, a business plan can become a collection of disconnected ideas, lacking the coherence necessary to inspire confidence in stakeholders or guide your own actions. To ensure alignment, it is important to articulate your vision early in the planning process and revisit it regularly as you craft each section of your plan. Consider a hypothetical entrepreneur whose vision is to "revolutionize education by making learning accessible to every child, regardless of their location or socioeconomic background." This statement, though broad, provides a guiding principle that informs every aspect of their business plan. Their market analysis will focus on underserved regions, their marketing strategy will prioritize outreach to schools and parents in those areas, and their financial projections will account for affordable pricing models or partnerships with nonprofit organizations. The vision acts as a compass, ensuring that every detail in the plan points toward a common destination.

Goals, on the other hand, provide the specificity needed to operationalize your vision. While the vision captures the overarching purpose of your business, goals break it down into measurable and actionable objectives. They serve as benchmarks for success, allowing you to track progress and make adjustments as needed. To align your business plan with your goals, it is important to define them clearly and ensure that every section of the plan contributes to achieving them.

One effective framework for setting goals is the SMART criteria: Specific, Measurable, Achievable, Relevant, and Time-bound. For example, instead of a vague goal like "increase sales," a SMART goal might be "increase monthly sales revenue by 15% within the next six months through targeted digital marketing campaigns." This level of specificity makes it easier to craft strategies that directly support the goal and to evaluate the success of those strategies over time. When aligning your business plan with your goals, it is also important to consider the different types of goals your business might have. Financial goals, such as achieving profitability or securing funding, are often the most obvious, but they are not the only ones that matter. Operational goals, such as streamlining production processes or expanding into new markets, play a critical role in long-term success. Similarly, customer-centric goals, like improving satisfaction scores or increasing retention rates, can drive growth and build brand loyalty. A well-aligned business plan addresses these diverse goals, weaving them into a unified strategy that supports your vision.

Alignment between your vision, goals, and business plan requires more than just stating them in the introduction; it demands consistency across every section. If your vision emphasizes sustainability, this should be reflected not only in your product design but also in your sourcing practices, marketing messaging, and even financial projections. Investors or partners reading your plan should see a clear thread that ties your vision to your goals and the strategies you have outlined to achieve them.

Achieving this consistency often involves revisiting and refining your plan as you go. You might start with a broad goal of "expand market share," but as you delve into your market analysis, you discover a specific niche where your product has the greatest potential. This insight allows you to refine the goal, aligning it more closely with your vision and ensuring that your strategies are well-targeted.

One of the challenges of aligning your business plan with your vision and goals is striking the right balance between ambition and realism. A compelling vision often requires bold aspirations, but a business plan grounded in reality is more likely to inspire confidence in stakeholders and guide effective decision-making. To achieve this balance, it is helpful to conduct a thorough assessment of your current resources, capabilities, and constraints. This assessment not only informs the feasibility of your goals but also helps you prioritize them based on their impact and achievability.

Flexibility is another important aspect of alignment. While your vision should remain a steadfast guiding light, your goals and strategies may need to evolve as circumstances change. Market conditions, customer needs, and competitive landscapes are rarely static, and a rigid business plan can quickly become obsolete. To maintain alignment, it is important to view your business plan as a living document, one that can be updated and adapted as new information becomes available. Alignment also requires a strong sense of personal connection to your vision and goals. As an entrepreneur, you are the driving force behind your business, and your passion and commitment must shine through every aspect of your plan. Stakeholders are not just investing in an idea; they are investing in your ability to execute that idea. A business plan that authentically reflects your vision and goals conveys not only the potential of your business but also your determination to see it succeed.

Ensuring your business plan aligns with your vision and goals is not a one-time effort; it is an ongoing process that requires regular reflection and adjustment. As your business grows and evolves, new opportunities and challenges will arise, and your vision and goals may need to adapt accordingly. Revisiting your business plan periodically allows you to assess whether it still reflects your current priorities and to make any necessary adjustments.

Crafting this document is not a linear process as it can be fraught with challenges. Whether you're writing your first business plan or refining an existing one, obstacles will inevitably arise, testing your commitment, creativity, and strategic thinking. However, recognizing these challenges and learning how to navigate them is crucial for ensuring that your business plan is not only comprehensive but also realistic, actionable, and sustainable. In this section, we explore some of the most common hurdles entrepreneurs face when creating their business plans and offer strategies for overcoming them.

One of the first challenges many entrepreneurs encounter is the inherent difficulty in predicting the future. Business plans, by their nature, require forecasting which is the ability to anticipate market trends, customer behavior, and financial outcomes in an ever-changing landscape. The level of uncertainty surrounding these projections can often lead to a sense of paralysis or frustration. While it is impossible to predict every variable with precision, it is important to strike a balance between optimism and realism.

A key strategy for managing uncertainty is to adopt a data-driven approach. In the early stages of writing your business plan, invest time in gathering as much relevant data as possible. This can include market research, customer surveys, competitor analysis, and industry reports. While no set of data will ever provide a perfect prediction, basing your forecasts on solid evidence rather than assumptions increases the likelihood that your projections will be grounded in reality. Additionally, being transparent about the assumptions underlying your projections allows investors, partners, and other stakeholders to understand the risks involved.

Another way to navigate uncertainty is through scenario planning. This involves imagining different possible futures and planning for each one. By considering multiple potential outcomes both positive and negative you can create contingency plans that help you respond quickly to unforeseen challenges. For example, your financial projections might include a best-case scenario, a worst-case scenario, and a moderate-growth scenario, each with corresponding strategies for managing the business in different environments. This approach not only provides clarity but also reassures stakeholders that you're prepared for uncertainty.

Beyond uncertainty, another common challenge in business planning is resource limitations. Many entrepreneurs face the reality that their resources whether capital, time, or manpower is limited, especially in the early stages of a business. This constraint can make it difficult to balance ambitious goals with the practical realities of what can be achieved with the available resources. The key to overcoming resource limitations is prioritization. Focus on the most critical areas that will have the greatest impact on your business's success. Instead of trying to do everything at once, create a phased approach that allows you to build momentum while managing resource constraints. A lean approach, where you focus on maximizing efficiency and minimizing unnecessary expenditures, can help ensure that you make the most of every penny, especially when funds are limited. Equally important is the need to secure adequate funding, which is often one of the most daunting aspects of business planning. Whether you are seeking loans, investors, or grants, presenting a well-thought-out business plan is essential for convincing potential backers that your business is worth the investment. This is where the importance of a strong executive summary, detailed market analysis, and realistic financial projections comes into play. By showing that you have a clear vision and a feasible path to profitability, you increase the chances of securing the funding you need to turn your business plan into reality.

Another significant challenge in business planning is maintaining focus amidst the overwhelming number of variables to consider. Entrepreneurs are often pulled in many directions, from product development to marketing to hiring staff. With so many moving parts, it can be easy to lose sight of the core objectives of your business plan. To navigate this challenge, it's essential to establish clear priorities and maintain a disciplined focus on your goals. One effective way to do this is through the use of key performance indicators (KPIs) which are measurable values that indicate how well your business is achieving its goals. KPIs, help you maintain focus by providing concrete metrics for success and enabling you to track your progress over time. Whether your goal is increasing sales revenue, improving customer satisfaction, or reducing operational costs, KPIs can help you stay aligned with your strategic objectives.

Creating a detailed action plan with timelines and deadlines can help you break down your business plan into manageable tasks. This approach helps to prevent overwhelm and ensures that each component of your plan is executed with precision. A clear action plan also allows you to measure progress and identify areas where adjustments may be needed.

While navigating the complexities of business planning, one of the most overlooked challenges is the emotional and psychological toll it can take on an entrepreneur. Writing a business plan often forces entrepreneurs to confront uncomfortable truths about their limitations, vulnerabilities, and the harsh realities of the market. This process can stir up feelings of doubt, fear, and even imposter syndrome. Overcoming this challenge requires mental resilience and a willingness to embrace failure as a learning experience. Rather than viewing obstacles as insurmountable, try to reframe them as opportunities for growth. Every setback provides valuable lessons that can inform your decisions moving forward. Additionally, seeking mentorship or support from fellow entrepreneurs can help you navigate the emotional highs and lows of business planning. Surrounding yourself with a supportive community can provide the encouragement and perspective you need to stay motivated and focused on your goals.

Another challenge that arises when crafting a business plan is the difficulty of articulating a unique value proposition (UVP) that differentiates your business from competitors. With countless businesses vying for attention in crowded markets, it is essential to establish a clear and compelling reason why customers should choose your product or service over others. Developing a strong UVP requires deep market research, an understanding of customer pain points, and a creative approach to problem-solving. The goal is to identify a gap in the market and position your business as the solution. Whether it's through innovation, cost-effectiveness, superior customer service, or a unique product feature, your UVP should be the thread that ties together your business's mission, vision, and goals. Once articulated clearly in your business plan, your UVP serves as a guiding force that informs your marketing, branding, and sales strategies.

Ultimately, overcoming these challenges requires a mindset of adaptability and perseverance. Business planning is not a static task but a dynamic process that evolves as you learn and grow. By approaching the process with patience, flexibility, and a commitment to continuous improvement, you can navigate the obstacles that come your way and build a business plan that not only sets the foundation for success but also empowers you to overcome future challenges.

CHAPTER FIVE
FUNDING THE DREAM: HOW TO SECURE RESOURCES FOR YOUR BUSINESS

Securing financial resources is one of the most critical steps in turning your vision into reality. Before diving into the mechanics of fundraising, it's essential to first understand your funding needs and the available options. This process requires a careful assessment of what your business requires to operate and grow, paired with a strategic exploration of the financial avenues that best align with your goals and circumstances.

The first step in understanding your funding needs is to analyze your business's financial requirements comprehensively. This involves breaking down your business plan into actionable components and attaching realistic costs to each. For instance, if you're launching a product-based business, you'll need to account for research and development, manufacturing, inventory, marketing, and distribution costs. For service-based businesses, you may need to consider personnel, training, marketing, and technology infrastructure. These costs, both one-time and recurring, create a detailed picture of the capital required to establish and sustain operations. Consider the stages of your business journey and how funding needs will evolve over time. The financial requirements of a startup in its early stages differ significantly from those of a growing or mature business. Early-stage businesses often require seed capital to develop prototypes, conduct market research, and establish an initial presence. As the business grows, the focus may shift to scaling operations, expanding into new markets, or refining the product or service offering. Anticipating these shifts allows you to plan your funding strategy proactively, rather than reacting to financial shortfalls.

Once you have a clear understanding of your funding needs, the next step is to explore the various funding options available. Broadly speaking, these options fall into three categories: personal financing, debt financing, and equity financing. Each option has unique characteristics, benefits, and challenges that make it suitable for different types of businesses and entrepreneurs.

Personal financing is often the first and most accessible source of funding for entrepreneurs. This includes using personal savings, leveraging assets, or relying on family and friends for financial support. While personal financing can demonstrate your commitment to your business and provide a quick start, it also carries significant risks. Tapping into personal savings or borrowing from loved ones can strain relationships and personal finances if the business doesn't perform as expected. Therefore, it's crucial to approach personal financing with a clear understanding of the risks involved and a plan for mitigating them.

Debt financing, which involves borrowing money that must be repaid with interest, is another common funding option. This category includes bank loans, small business loans, and lines of credit. This financing allows you to retain full ownership of your business while accessing the capital needed to grow. However, it also requires a steady revenue stream to meet repayment obligations, which can be challenging for businesses in their early stages. Lenders often require a solid business plan, collateral, and a strong credit history, making it essential to prepare thoroughly before seeking debt financing.

Equity financing, on the other hand, involves raising capital by selling shares of your business to investors. This approach is popular among startups and high-growth companies that require significant funding to scale. Equity financing provides access to large amounts of capital without the burden of repayment, but it comes at the cost of sharing ownership and decision-making power. Common sources of equity financing include angel investors, venture capital firms, and crowdfunding platforms. To attract equity investors, you need to demonstrate not only the potential for strong returns but also the unique value your business brings to the market.

Each funding option also comes with its own set of expectations and timelines. For example, banks and traditional lenders often focus on financial stability and the ability to repay loans, while venture capitalists prioritize high growth potential and scalability. Crowd-funding platforms, on the other hand, rely on public interest and engagement. Understanding the specific criteria and expectations of each funding source is critical to choosing the right one for your business. In addition to these traditional funding options, emerging financial tools and platforms have expanded the range of possibilities for entrepreneurs. Peer-to-peer lending platforms, for example, allow businesses to borrow money directly from individuals, bypassing traditional banks. Similarly, government grants and subsidies can provide non-repayable funding for businesses operating in priority sectors, such as technology, renewable energy, or community development. These options can be particularly appealing for entrepreneurs looking to minimize debt or equity dilution.

Choosing the right funding source is not just about meeting immediate financial needs but also entails aligning with your long-term vision and values. For instance, if maintaining control of your business is a top priority, you may prefer debt financing over equity financing. Conversely, if you're focused on rapid growth and willing to share ownership, equity financing may be a better fit. The decision should also consider the level of involvement you want from your financers. Angel investors and venture capitalists often bring valuable expertise, networks, and mentorship, but their involvement can also mean giving up some control over business decisions.

Understanding your funding options also requires an awareness of the broader economic environment and how it impacts access to capital. Economic conditions, interest rates, and investor sentiment can all influence the availability and cost of funding. During periods of economic uncertainty, lenders may tighten credit requirements, making it harder to secure loans. Similarly, investors may become more risk-averse, focusing on businesses with proven track records and steady cash flows. Staying informed about these external factors can help you time your fundraising efforts strategically and adjust your approach as needed.

Another critical consideration is the legal and regulatory framework surrounding different funding options. Each source of capital comes with its own set of rules and obligations, from interest rates and repayment terms to shareholder agreements and compliance requirements. Failing to understand these obligations can lead to financial and legal complications down the road. Equity financing often requires detailed documentation, including shareholder agreements, valuation reports, and compliance with securities laws. Working with legal and financial advisors can help you navigate these complexities and ensure that your funding arrangements are transparent and well-structured.

As you explore funding options, it's important to remember that securing financial resources is not just about raising money, it's about building relationships. Whether you're approaching a bank, pitching to investors, or engaging with a crowdfunding audience, your ability to connect with your audience and communicate your vision is key to success. This involves more than just presenting numbers and projections; it requires telling a compelling story that inspires confidence and excitement about your business.

When pitching to investors, focus on the problem your business solves, the market opportunity, and the unique value your solution brings. Use data and evidence to back up your claims, but don't underestimate the power of passion and authenticity. Investors want to see that you not only have a great idea but also the drive and resilience to make it a reality. Similarly, when engaging with audiences, emphasize the impact your business will have on their lives or the community. Personal stories and relatable narratives can go a long way in building trust and enthusiasm. By taking the time to assess your requirements, explore your options, and choose the right approach, you can lay a solid foundation for securing the resources you need to build and grow your business. Whether you're launching a startup or scaling an established venture, this understanding is the first step toward funding your dream and turning your entrepreneurial aspirations into reality.

When it comes to securing financial resources for your entrepreneurial venture, crafting a compelling pitch for investors is one of the most crucial steps. A well-prepared pitch is not just about presenting numbers and financial projections; it is about telling a story that captures the essence of your business, showcases its potential, and instills confidence in those you are asking to invest in your vision. Whether your audience consists of angel investors, venture capitalists, or even family and friends, the quality of your pitch can make or break your funding efforts.

The foundation of a successful pitch is a deep understanding of your business, the market you are operating in, and the specific needs of your target audience. Investors want to know that you have a clear grasp of the problem your business is solving, the size of the opportunity, and how your solution is uniquely positioned to succeed. This begins with articulating a problem that resonates. The problem should not only be significant but also relatable to the investors. If you can connect the problem to a personal story or a larger trend, it becomes easier to make a compelling case for why your solution is worth backing.

Once the problem is clear, the next step is to highlight your solution. This is your chance to showcase the uniqueness of your product or service. What sets it apart from existing options? How does it provide value in a way that competitors cannot? Whether it's an innovative technology, a proprietary process, or a game-changing customer experience, your solution should stand out as the ideal answer to the problem you've identified. The more specific and evidence-based your explanation, the more credible your pitch will be. A key element of a persuasive pitch is a thorough understanding of your target market. Investors want to see that you've done your homework and can confidently describe the size and dynamics of the market you're entering. This includes not only quantifying the market opportunity but also segmenting it to show where your business fits in. For example, if you are launching a product aimed at millennials, you should be able to detail their purchasing behaviors, preferences, and how your product aligns with their needs. The more precise your market insights, the more convincing your pitch will be.

Financial projections play a central role in any pitch. Investors are inherently focused on returns, so you must demonstrate that your business has the potential to generate significant financial value. This involves presenting clear, realistic revenue forecasts, profit margins, and cash flow projections. However, it is not enough to simply throw numbers onto a slide. You must explain the assumptions behind your projections and connect them to relatable data. If you predict rapid growth in your first three years, you should be able to point to industry benchmarks, early customer feedback, or pilot results that support your optimism.

While financial projections are critical, it is equally important to acknowledge risks and challenges. No investor expects a business to be free of obstacles. In fact, addressing potential risks upfront and demonstrating a plan to mitigate them can build trust and credibility. Whether it is competition, regulatory hurdles, or operational complexities, showing that you've thought about and prepared for challenges reassures investors that you are realistic and capable of navigating difficulties.

Another crucial component of a strong pitch is the team behind the business. Investors don't just invest in ideas; they invest in people. Highlighting the strengths of your team, including their expertise, experience, and passion, is essential. If your team has a track record of success, make sure to emphasize it. If there are gaps in expertise, acknowledge them and explain how you plan to address them, whether through hiring, partnerships, or advisory roles. A strong team can inspire confidence even in cases where the business idea is still in its early stages.

Your pitch should also outline a clear business model. Investors need to understand how your business plans to make money and how it will sustain profitability over time. This includes detailing your revenue streams, pricing strategy, and cost structure. A transparent and well-thought-out business model signal to investors that you've considered the practical aspects of running and scaling your venture.

Storytelling is another powerful tool in crafting a compelling pitch. Numbers and data are important, but stories are what truly resonate with people. A well-told story can humanize your business, make it memorable, and create an emotional connection with investors. Whether it's the story of how you came up with your business idea, a testimonial from a customer, or an anecdote that illustrates the impact of your product, incorporating narrative elements into your pitch can make it more engaging and persuasive.

While the content of your pitch is vital, its delivery is equally important. Investors will judge not only what you say but also how you say it. Confidence, clarity, and enthusiasm are key to making a positive impression. Practice your pitch repeatedly, refine it based on feedback, and ensure that you can deliver it seamlessly within the allotted time. Avoid overloading your presentation with jargon or unnecessary details. Instead, focus on communicating your key points clearly and concisely. Visual aids, such as slides or prototypes, can also enhance your pitch, but they should complement your message rather than distract from it.

Building relationships with investors is another critical aspect of pitching. Rarely will an investor commit to funding your business after a single presentation. The pitch is often just the beginning of a longer conversation. Take the time to build rapport, understand the investor's priorities, and address their concerns. This might involve follow-up meetings, providing additional data, or even adjusting your approach based on their feedback. Demonstrating that you are open to collaboration and willing to listen can go a long way in fostering trust and securing investment.

Understanding your audience is essential to tailoring your pitch effectively. Different investors have different priorities, and your pitch should reflect this. For example, angel investors may be more interested in your personal story and passion for the business, while venture capitalists may focus on scalability and market potential. Similarly, if you are pitching to impact investors, emphasize the social or environmental benefits of your business. The more you can align your pitch with the values and interests of your audience, the more persuasive it will be. Be prepared for questions and objections. No matter how polished your pitch is, investors will want to probe deeper into your assumptions, plans, and projections. Anticipate potential questions and practice your responses. This includes not only addressing factual queries but also handling challenging or skeptical comments with professionalism and poise. Being well-prepared shows that you take the process seriously and increases your credibility.

Bootstrapping (Self-Funding) and Financial Management for Sustainability

When embarking on the entrepreneurial journey, many find that external funding is either unavailable or undesirable. In such cases, self-financing becomes not only a necessity but also a strategic choice that can lay the groundwork for financial independence and long-term sustainability. This approach demands discipline, resourcefulness, and a strong commitment to building a lean and efficient business model.

Relying on personal resources, reinvested profits, and creative problem-solving, rather than relying on external investors, allows entrepreneurs to retain full control of their businesses. This autonomy enables decision-making that aligns directly with the founder's vision, without the pressures of meeting investor expectations or external timelines. However, this independence comes with its own set of challenges, as the constraints of limited capital often require founders to stretch their resources and make significant sacrifices.

A self-funded approach begins with a frugal mindset. Entrepreneurs must carefully evaluate every expense to ensure it directly contributes to business growth. This might involve operating out of a home office instead of renting space, using free or low-cost software tools, or hiring freelance workers instead of full-time employees. Negotiating better deals with suppliers, outsourcing non-core activities, and embracing a do-it-yourself attitude wherever feasible are all strategies that help keep costs low. By focusing on efficiency, self-funded businesses can reduce financial strain while still achieving incremental progress.

A critical aspect of this financial approach is identifying and securing early revenue streams. Generating income as soon as possible not only provides much-needed cash flow but also validates the business model and its potential for scalability. This often involves launching a minimum viable product (MVP) or offering a pared-down version of the service to start attracting customers. For instance, a tech startup might release a beta version of its software with limited features, while a physical product business might offer pre-orders or prototypes. These initial offerings serve as both revenue drivers and opportunities to gather customer feedback for improvement.

This strategy also encourages creativity in marketing and customer acquisition. Without the budget for extensive advertising campaigns, founders must rely on low-cost or non-cost marketing strategies to build awareness and attract customers. Social media platforms, content marketing, and word-of-mouth referrals have become invaluable tools. Hosting events, networking, and forming strategic partnerships can also help businesses reach new audiences without significant financial investment. By leveraging personal networks and community connections, self-funded entrepreneurs can achieve meaningful growth on a tight budget. Despite its many advantages, this independent approach is not without its risks and limitations. Relying solely on personal or internal resources can lead to financial strain, especially if the business encounters unexpected challenges or slower-than-anticipated growth. Founders may need to forego salaries, take on personal debt, or delay significant life milestones to keep their businesses afloat. These sacrifices can take a toll on mental and emotional well-being, making it essential for self-financed entrepreneurs to practice self-care and seek support when needed.

To mitigate these risks, effective financial management is critical. This begins with meticulous budgeting and forecasting. Entrepreneurs must track every expense, anticipate future costs, and plan for cash flow fluctuations. Tools such as accounting software, spreadsheets, and financial dashboards can simplify this process, providing valuable insights into the business's financial health. Setting aside reserves for emergencies, negotiating flexible payment terms with suppliers, and diversifying revenue streams are additional steps that can help safeguard the business against unforeseen difficulties.

Another important aspect of financial management is understanding and monitoring key performance indicators (KPIs). Metrics such as customer acquisition cost (CAC), lifetime value (LTV), gross margin, and cash flow are essential for evaluating the business's financial performance and making informed decisions. For example, if the CAC exceeds the LTV, it may indicate that marketing efforts are inefficient or that the product pricing needs adjustment. Regularly reviewing and analyzing these metrics enables founders to identify issues early and take corrective action. As the business grows, self-financed entrepreneurs often face the challenge of scaling with limited resources. Growth typically requires additional investments in personnel, infrastructure, and marketing, which can strain existing finances. To address this, many self-funded businesses adopt incremental scaling strategies, focusing on gradual expansion rather than rapid growth. By aligning growth efforts with available resources, businesses can maintain financial stability while pursuing expansion opportunities.

In some cases, self-funded businesses may eventually choose to seek external funding to support scaling efforts. However, the experience of operating lean often positions these businesses to negotiate from a place of strength. Having achieved profitability or established a loyal customer base, self-financed entrepreneurs can demonstrate their ability to manage resources effectively and deliver results. This track record can make them more attractive to investors and lenders, allowing them to secure favorable terms.

It also fosters a culture of innovation and adaptability. The constraints of limited financing often push entrepreneurs to find creative solutions to problems, whether through process improvements, cost-saving measures, or alternative business models. This resourcefulness can become a competitive advantage, enabling the business to thrive even in challenging market conditions. Moreover, the focus on efficiency and customer value that self-financing necessitates often leads to the development of products and services that are highly aligned with market needs. Another advantage of self-financing is the ability to build a business that is fundamentally sustainable. Without the pressure to achieve rapid growth or meet investor expectations, these businesses can prioritize long-term stability and profitability over short-term gains. This often results in healthier financial foundations, lower risk profiles, and greater resilience during economic downturns. Retaining full ownership allows founders to maintain control over the business's direction and vision, ensuring that decisions are driven by mission and values rather than external pressures.

However, it is important for self-financed entrepreneurs to recognize the limits of self-reliance and seek external expertise when necessary. This might involve hiring financial advisors, working with mentors, or joining entrepreneurial networks to gain insights and support. Accessing knowledge and resources from outside the business can help founders avoid costly mistakes and identify opportunities for improvement. By balancing self-reliance with collaboration, self-financed businesses can strengthen their foundations and enhance their chances of success.

Self-funding and financial management are cornerstones of sustainable entrepreneurship. While this approach requires significant discipline, creativity, and sacrifice, it also offers unique advantages, including full ownership, financial independence, and a strong focus on efficiency and value creation. By embracing a lean mindset, prioritizing early revenue generation, and practicing effective financial management, entrepreneurs can navigate the challenges of self-financing and build resilient, thriving businesses. Whether pursued as a long-term strategy or a steppingstone to external funding, self-financing empowers founders to take control of their financial destinies and achieve their entrepreneurial dreams on their own terms.

CHAPTER SIX
BUILDING CONNECTIONS THAT MATTER

Mentorship is a vital pillar to last and succeed in this industry. For many successful entrepreneurs, the wisdom and guidance offered by mentors have played a significant role in shaping their business trajectory. A mentor provides much more than advice; they offer perspective, challenge assumptions, and help navigate complex decisions, often leveraging years of experience to help the mentee avoid costly mistakes. As an entrepreneur, it is essential to recognize the value of mentorship and to actively seek mentors who can foster growth, offer constructive feedback, and help you refine your vision for the business.

In its simplest form, mentorship is a relationship between an experienced individual (the mentor) and someone seeking guidance (the mentee). However, the benefits of mentorship extend far beyond this basic dynamic. Mentorship is about leveraging the knowledge, experience, and networks of more seasoned individuals to accelerate your personal and professional growth. For entrepreneurs, it can provide invaluable insights into various aspects of business, from refining a product or service offering to developing leadership skills and making strategic decisions.

The impact of mentorship on entrepreneurship cannot be overstated. One of the first and most significant ways in which a mentor can help is by guiding you through the early stages of building your business. As a new entrepreneur, you are bound to face many obstacles, including navigating financial planning, dealing with the complexities of legal and regulatory requirements, and setting up operational processes. A mentor, especially one who has walked this path before, can share lessons learned from their own experiences, ensuring that you avoid common mistakes and make informed decisions. This knowledge becomes a shortcut to success, helping you save time, money, and effort by allowing you to avoid repeating the errors of others.

Mentors can also offer objective perspectives, helping you make difficult decisions with a clear, unbiased view. As an entrepreneur, you will inevitably face moments of uncertainty whether it's pivoting your business model, dealing with unexpected challenges, or deciding how to grow the company. During these moments, having a mentor who has a long-term perspective, and an understanding of the business landscape can make all the difference. They can help you reflect on the broader vision of your company, assess the risks, and suggest viable strategies that you may not have considered. This type of support can ease the burden of decision-making and provide a sense of confidence, knowing that you have a trusted advisor by your side. Another valuable contribution a mentor can make is helping you expand your professional network. A mentor, particularly one with a wealth of experience in your industry, often has access to networks, resources, and opportunities that may otherwise be difficult to reach. Through their connections, they can introduce you to potential partners, investors, clients, and collaborators, thus expanding your reach and opening doors for your business.

They often act as references or advocates for you within their own professional networks, which can be especially helpful when seeking funding, clients, or strategic alliances. Building a network through mentorship can also provide invaluable insights into industry trends, new technologies, and emerging market opportunities that may give your business a competitive edge.

Another aspect is the opportunity to gain insight into leadership development. As an entrepreneur, you will eventually be required to lead a team, manage resources, and make decisions that affect not only the future of your business but the livelihoods of your employees. Having a mentor who has navigated the challenges of leadership can be extremely beneficial. A mentor can help you refine your leadership style, offering tips on effective communication, decision-making, and team building. They can also help you navigate the emotional and psychological challenges of leadership, providing advice on how to stay resilient, manage stress, and maintain a clear vision despite adversity. They can be a sounding board for leadership challenges, helping you develop the emotional intelligence required to successfully lead and inspire your team.

Furthermore, it can also support personal development, which is often just as important as business growth. Entrepreneurs are typically high achievers who are passionate about their businesses, but it can be easy to overlook the personal challenges that come with entrepreneurship. A mentor provides a safe space to discuss fears, challenges, and personal aspirations. This space can be essential for avoiding burnout, making better work-life balance decisions, and remaining focused on long-term personal and professional goals. It is not just about business advice but about growing as a person, developing confidence, understanding your strengths and weaknesses, and learning how to navigate life's challenges while building a business.

Finding the right mentor is essential to ensuring a productive and mutually beneficial relationship. While the concept of mentorship might seem straightforward, the process of identifying, building, and nurturing a mentor-mentee relationship requires care and intentionality. The best mentors are those who align with your values, understand your goals, and are genuinely interested in your success. It is important to seek individuals who are not only experts in your field but also those who are invested in personal growth and open to sharing their knowledge. When looking for a mentor, consider both technical expertise and interpersonal chemistry because mentorship is most effective when there is mutual respect, trust, and a sense of shared purpose.

It is also essential to understand the different types of mentorships that can be beneficial at various stages of your entrepreneurial journey. The most common type of mentor-mentee relationship is one-on-one mentoring, where the mentor provides guidance and advice tailored to the mentee's specific business needs. However, there are other forms of mentorship as well, such as group mentoring, where a group of entrepreneurs or business owners meet with one or more experienced mentors to discuss business challenges, share insights, and learn from each other's experiences. Group mentoring can be an excellent way to gain diverse perspectives on a particular issue while simultaneously expanding your network. Peer mentoring is another valuable form of mentorship where individuals with similar experiences collaborate and provide guidance to one another. Peer mentors can offer support that is more in tune with the immediate challenges faced by a growing business and can often relate more directly to the unique difficulties you may be experiencing.

The mentoring process is not one-sided, it is a partnership. As a mentee, you must be willing to put in the effort, be open to feedback, and take responsibility for your own growth. Effective mentees are proactive in seeking advice, demonstrating a willingness to learn, and following through suggestions made by their mentors. They are also open to constructive criticism, using it as an opportunity for growth rather than as a personal attack. Successful mentoring relationships are built on trust, respect, and a shared commitment to learning. Both parties must be willing to invest time and energy into the relationship for it to flourish.

Moreover, the role of mentorship does not end once the business reaches a certain level of success. In fact, as your business grows, your mentoring needs may evolve. You may outgrow a mentor who is focused on the early stages of entrepreneurship and may need to seek out more advanced guidance as your business enters new phases of growth. Likewise, as you gain experience and expertise, you may find yourself in a position to nurture others, passing on the knowledge and wisdom that you have gained. The cycle of mentorship is a two-way street, while you learn from those who have gone before you, you also have the opportunity to give back and help others navigate their own entrepreneurial journeys.

It is an invaluable resource for any entrepreneur seeking to grow their business. The guidance, perspective, and support that mentors provide can accelerate growth, help you make better decisions, and expand your personal and professional networks. More than just business advice, mentorship nurtures leadership, personal development, and resilience, qualities that are essential for sustainable success. To maximize the benefits, it is important to seek persons who align with your goals, values, and vision. By building strong mentor-mentee relationships, entrepreneurs can navigate the complex challenges of starting and growing a business with greater confidence, insight, and success.

In the business world, success is often determined not just by individual effort but by the ability to collaborate effectively with others. While technical skills, creativity, and dedication are essential for entrepreneurial success, the ability to leverage relationships with other organizations or individuals can make all the difference. These relationships are often formalized through partnerships, which allow entrepreneurs to combine their resources, expertise, and market access to scale their businesses more effectively. The concept of collaboration is at the heart of many successful business ventures, and understanding how to identify, form, and manage these relationships is crucial for anyone aiming to grow their business.

A partnership is a powerful tool for businesses, providing the opportunity to share resources, ideas, and expertise. By partnering with a business or organization that brings complementary skills, you gain access to additional capabilities that you might not have in-house. This could include technology, distribution networks, expertise, or even local market knowledge. For smaller businesses, partnering with a larger, more established company can level the playing field, providing the resources needed to compete with bigger players.

When identifying potential partners, it's essential to focus on businesses or organizations whose strengths complement your own. A successful partnership should be based on a foundation of mutual benefit as each partner should bring something of value to the table. This value can take many forms, from technical expertise and innovation to access to new customer bases or distribution channels.

One of the first steps to forming a successful partnership is identifying businesses or individuals who share similar values, goals, and objectives. The alignment of vision and mission ensures that both sides are working toward the same long-term objectives and can make joint decisions with confidence. A partner whose goals differ drastically from yours may lead to conflicts or misunderstandings down the line. Therefore, it is crucial to establish a shared vision early on in the relationship, setting clear expectations from the start.

Once the right potential partner is identified, the next step is to establish a strong foundation of trust. Trust is the bedrock of any successful partnership. Without it, communication breaks down, conflicts arise, and the partnership is likely to fail. Building trust involves being transparent about goals, capabilities, and expectations. Having open, honest conversations about each party's strengths, weaknesses, and limitations is essential for setting realistic expectations and ensuring that both sides feel confident in the partnership. Trust is not built overnight, but rather developed through ongoing communication, collaboration, and accountability.

As partnerships are about sharing resources, establishing clear agreements and legal structures from the beginning is important. Every partnership should have a formal agreement that outlines roles, responsibilities, and the expectations of each party. This includes defining how profits will be shared, intellectual property will be managed, and how the partnership will operate day-to-day. The legal agreement should also detail the terms for resolving conflicts, as well as a clear exit strategy in case the relationship no longer works. A well-structured agreement minimizes potential misunderstandings and conflicts, providing a framework for the partnership to function smoothly.

They can come in many forms, and the type of partnership chosen will depend on the needs of the business and the objectives of the entrepreneurs involved. One common type of partnership is a joint venture, in which two or more businesses come together to create a new entity. This new entity might focus on a specific project or market, with each partner contributing resources such as capital, technology, or market knowledge. Joint ventures are especially effective for expanding into new markets or launching new products that neither party could effectively tackle alone. By combining resources, partners can mitigate risks, share the costs of development, and increase the chances of success.

Another type of partnership is a distribution or marketing alliance. In these partnerships, one business provides its products or services to be marketed and sold by another company. This kind of relationship is particularly useful for companies that want to expand their reach but don't have the necessary infrastructure or resources to do so on their own. For instance, a business in one country may partner with a distributor in another country to enter the new market without having to establish its own physical presence. The distributor benefits from access to unique products, while the business expands its market presence without the upfront costs.

Technology partnerships are increasingly popular as innovation becomes a key driver of business success. In these partnerships, businesses join forces with technology companies to integrate advanced tools, platforms, or software into their products or services. This can be a game-changer for businesses that want to leverage the latest technologies but lack the resources or expertise to build them internally. By partnering with a technology provider, businesses can access top-notch tools that improve their offerings and provide better value to their customers.

Besides forming partnerships with other businesses, entrepreneurs can also look to connect with nonprofit organizations, research institutions, or government agencies. These kinds of relationships can open up new avenues for funding, research collaboration, and access to networks. For instance, a partnership with an academic institution might give your business access to specialized research or emerging technology, while collaboration with a government agency might provide opportunities for funding or public-sector contracts. These relationships can be invaluable, particularly for businesses in the early stages of development, as they provide additional resources and credibility that can accelerate growth.

Strategic partnerships can also provide opportunities for risk-sharing. Expanding into new markets or launching new products involves inherent risks, but these risks can be mitigated by partnering with another business. By sharing the risks and rewards, businesses can move forward with greater confidence. It also allows businesses to pool their financial resources, which can help them manage the costs of market expansion more effectively.

Even with all the benefits that come with collaboration, entrepreneurs must remain aware of the risks that partnerships can bring. Misaligned goals, incompatible cultures, or unclear expectations can result in conflict or the dissolution of the partnership. This is why it is so important to have clear, upfront agreements in place and to monitor the partnership's health over time. Regular check-ins and open communication are essential for ensuring that both parties remain aligned and that the partnership continues to deliver value. Entrepreneurs should also be prepared to make adjustments or even end the partnership if it is no longer serving the business's best interests.

Moreover, while partnerships can offer numerous benefits, it is essential for entrepreneurs to maintain control over their business and its direction. While collaborating with others is crucial, it is important not to relinquish too much control or allow partners to make decisions that could negatively affect the business. Founders should always protect their long-term vision and ensure that their business goals remain the top priority.

Strategic partnerships are an invaluable tool for entrepreneurs seeking to expand their reach, grow their businesses, and access resources and expertise they may not have on their own. By identifying the right partners, establishing trust, and forming mutually beneficial agreements, entrepreneurs can create relationships that accelerate growth and increase the chances of long-term success. While there are risks involved, the rewards of working such as shared resources, access to new markets, and enhanced innovation make these partnerships an essential element of any entrepreneur's growth strategy. By building and maintaining strong partnerships, entrepreneurs can set themselves up for long-term success and sustainable business growth.

Entrepreneurship is often portrayed as an individual journey, with the founder at the helm, making tough decisions and navigating challenges alone. However, the truth is that no entrepreneur succeeds in isolation. Behind every successful business is a network of people, partners, colleagues, customers, and supporters who contribute to its growth and success. Building a supportive ecosystem through community involvement is a vital part of entrepreneurship. The people you surround yourself with can offer insights, advice, emotional support, and even practical resources that can help elevate your business to the next level.

A strong community is built on relationships. These relationships span various sectors, from industry peers to potential customers, investors, and mentors. Each of these relationships plays a unique role in the entrepreneurial ecosystem, contributing to the overall success of the entrepreneur and the business. By engaging with a wide range of people and organizations, individuals can access different perspectives, discover new opportunities, and overcome challenges that might otherwise seem insurmountable.

Building a supportive system entails understanding the value of collaboration. In the early stages of a business, it is easy to feel the pressure of doing everything on your own from developing the product, handling marketing, managing operations, and so on. However, no one person can excel at every aspect of a business. The key to success lies in surrounding yourself with a group of talented individuals who can complement your skills and expertise. By collaborating with others, entrepreneurs can tap into a collective pool of knowledge and experience, resulting in better decision-making, improved problem-solving, and a stronger overall business. When building your ecosystem, it's important to recognize that community isn't just about what others can do for you but also about what you can contribute to the community. Entrepreneurs, who actively give back to the system, whether by offering advice, mentoring other entrepreneurs, or sharing knowledge, often find that they receive support in return. This sense of reciprocity helps create a thriving environment where everyone benefits. A community thrives when individuals and businesses support one another, share resources, and collaborate toward mutual goals.

In the digital age, building a community goes beyond local networks. Online platforms and social media have made it easier than ever to connect with like-minded entrepreneurs, potential customers, and business partners from around the world. Social media, in particular, offers founders a powerful tool for building relationships, sharing their stories, and promoting their businesses. Platforms like LinkedIn, Twitter, and industry-specific forums provide opportunities to connect with individuals and organizations that can help drive your business forward. Engaging with online communities allows entrepreneurs to learn from others, share their experiences, and even forge international partnerships that can help expand their reach and grow their businesses.

Being part of a supportive system also means engaging with organizations that offer resources and support to entrepreneurs. These can include incubators, accelerators, government programs, professional networks, and industry groups. Such organizations often provide access to funding, training, mentorship, and networking opportunities that can help entrepreneurs scale their businesses. By becoming involved in these communities, entrepreneurs can gain access to vital resources that can help them overcome common obstacles, refine their strategies, and stay ahead of industry trends.

Fostering creativity, a strong community also provides a safety net for entrepreneurs. The journey of building a business can be full of ups and downs and having a supportive group of people to rely on can help entrepreneurs navigate these challenges. Whether it's a colleague offering advice on how to solve a technical problem, a mentor helping to refine a business strategy, or a fellow entrepreneur providing moral support during tough times, a strong community acts as a source of encouragement and reassurance. This emotional support is especially important during difficult moments when entrepreneurs may feel overwhelmed or discouraged. Knowing that others have faced similar challenges and have overcome them can provide the motivation and confidence needed to push through adversity.

Furthermore, building a supportive system is essential for increasing visibility and credibility. In the early stages of a business, it can be difficult to attract attention and gain traction in the market. However, by becoming an active participant in a community, entrepreneurs can increase their visibility and establish their credibility. Whether it's through speaking at events, contributing to online forums, or sharing insights through blog posts and social media, engaging with the community helps build recognition and trust.

Another key benefit of building a community is the opportunity to receive constructive feedback. Running a business in a vacuum can lead to blind spots and missed opportunities. Engaging with other entrepreneurs, industry experts, and customers allows entrepreneurs to receive feedback on their products, services, and strategies. This feedback can be invaluable in refining the business, identifying areas for improvement, and avoiding costly mistakes. In some cases, feedback from the community may lead to new ideas for product development, marketing strategies, or business models that can help entrepreneurs stay ahead of the competition.

The value of community and building a supportive system cannot be overstated. Entrepreneurs who actively engage with their networks, seek mentorship, collaborate with peers, and contribute to their communities are better positioned for success. A strong ecosystem provides access to knowledge, resources, and opportunities that can help entrepreneurs navigate the complexities of business ownership. It fosters a culture of innovation, creativity, and problem-solving, while also offering emotional support and a sense of belonging. By building and nurturing these relationships, entrepreneurs can not only grow their businesses but also contribute to the success and growth of the broader entrepreneurial community. It is not a solitary journey but is a collective endeavor, and success is often achieved through the power of connection and collaboration.

CHAPTER SEVEN
SCALING SMARTLY

When a business begins to show signs of success, the natural inclination is to expand. Growth, while desirable, is not without its challenges. Expanding too quickly or without the proper framework can lead to operational inefficiencies, financial strain, or even failure. To navigate this phase effectively, entrepreneurs must establish a solid foundation to ensure that their enterprise grows in a sustainable and strategic manner.

Scaling a business prematurely is one of the most common pitfalls for new entrepreneurs. Expansion should not be driven solely by excitement or external pressure; it must be a calculated decision based on tangible evidence of readiness. This readiness can be measured by consistent revenue streams, robust customer demand, and operational stability. Consider a business that has just launched its flagship product. If demand spikes, it may be tempting to immediately invest in additional inventory, staff, or facilities. However, this decision must be backed by data. Are the sales figures part of a recurring trend, or are they influenced by a one-time event, such as a promotional campaign? Entrepreneurs must analyze their growth patterns to ensure that the demand they are experiencing is sustainable.

It is also necessary to consider timing as it involves more than just the business's internal metrics. External factors, such as market trends, economic conditions, and competitive landscape, must also be evaluated. A growing business must operate within the context of its industry. For instance, launching a new product during a recession might require a more cautious approach than during an economic boom. A critical aspect of preparing for growth is evaluating whether your current infrastructure can support it. Infrastructure, in this context, refers to the systems, processes, and tools that keep the business running smoothly. These could include technology platforms, supply chain logistics, and communication systems. Founders must assess their financial resources. Growth often requires significant capital investment, whether for hiring new employees, acquiring equipment, or marketing to a broader audience. Before scaling, it's vital to ensure that the business has a healthy cash flow and access to funding if needed. Bootstrapping might work in the initial stages, but growth often necessitates external financing, such as loans or investor support.

One of the most overlooked aspects of growth is the need for systems that can adapt to increased demand without collapsing. Scalable systems are those that maintain efficiency and effectiveness regardless of the volume of work or customers. Start by automating repetitive tasks. Automation tools, such as customer relationship management (CRM) software, payroll systems, or inventory management platforms, can save time and reduce errors. For instance, instead of manually tracking customer inquiries, businesses can implement a ticketing system that organizes and prioritizes requests. Standardizing processes is another key step. Documenting workflows and creating clear standard operating procedures (SOPs) ensures consistency even as the business grows.

Scalable systems also extend to the organizational structure. As the business grows, decision-making should not be concentrated on one person. Empowering team members with clearly defined roles and responsibilities fosters efficiency and prevents bottlenecks.

While it is essential to have structured systems and processes, flexibility should also be part of the growth strategy. The business environment is dynamic, and unexpected changes can disrupt even the best and most organized well-laid plans. For instance, during the COVID-19 pandemic, many businesses had to pivot their operations overnight. Restaurants that relied solely on in-house dining had to adapt to delivery and takeout models. Retail stores had to ramp up their online presence. These examples underscore the importance of being agile and prepared to shift strategies in response to external events. Entrepreneurs should regularly review their business plans and adjust them based on current realities. This iterative approach ensures that the business remains relevant and competitive, even in the face of uncertainty.

Fundamentally, the foundation for sustainable growth includes the mindset of the entrepreneur and their team. A growth-oriented culture encourages innovation, accountability, and resilience. Leaders must communicate the vision of growth clearly to their employees. When the team understands the goals and the rationale behind scaling, they are more likely to align their efforts with the company's objectives. Open communication channels, regular feedback, and recognition of contributions create a sense of ownership and commitment among employees. Moreover, fostering a culture of continuous learning is essential. As the business evolves, so must the skills and knowledge of its workforce. Providing opportunities for training, attending industry conferences, or encouraging employees to pursue certifications can help the team stay ahead of the curve.

Laying the groundwork for sustainable growth requires meticulous planning, a deep understanding of the business' strengths and limitations, and a willingness to adapt. By focusing on timing, infrastructure, scalable systems, and fostering a growth-oriented culture, entrepreneurs can position their businesses for long-term success. Scaling is not just about getting bigger but rather it's about growing better, ensuring that every step forward strengthens the foundation of the enterprise. This strategic approach not only minimizes risks but also maximizes the potential for success, allowing businesses to thrive in an ever-changing marketplace. Entrepreneurs who invest time and effort in building this foundation are more likely to navigate the complexities of growth with confidence and control.

Hiring and structuring the right team is one of the most pivotal aspects of scaling a business. As a company grows, the demands placed on its operations, leadership, and culture intensify, necessitating a team capable of meeting these new challenges. The team you build during this critical phase will largely determine how well your business can sustain its momentum, maintain its values, and capitalize on new opportunities. However, finding the right balance between expertise, adaptability, and cultural fit requires a thoughtful approach, as does structuring the organization to support effective communication and decision-making.

When expanding, many entrepreneurs fall into the trap of prioritizing rapid hiring over thoughtful hiring. It's easy to assume that the fastest way to address the challenges of growth is to bring in as many new employees as possible. Yet, indiscriminate hiring can lead to a bloated workforce, inefficiencies, and even conflict within the organization. Every new hire should address a specific need within the business. Identifying these needs requires clarity about the company's objectives and the gaps in the current team. For example, if a growing company is struggling to meet increasing demand for its product, hiring additional staff in operations or supply chain management may be a priority. On the other hand, if the issue lies in scaling sales efforts, the focus should shift to onboarding skilled sales professionals or marketing experts.

The key to making strategic hires lies in understanding both the technical skills required for a role and the interpersonal qualities that will allow the individual to thrive within the organization. Technical proficiency ensures that the employee can contribute immediately to their area of expertise, but interpersonal qualities like adaptability, teamwork, and alignment with the company's mission are equally important. During periods of rapid growth, businesses often face uncertainty and change. Employees who are adaptable and willing to embrace new challenges are more likely to succeed in this environment than those who rigidly adhere to a single way of working.

Cultural fitness is another crucial consideration when hiring for growth. Every business has its own unique culture, shaped by the values, behaviors, and norms of its founders and team members. As the organization grows, maintaining this culture becomes more challenging, yet it is essential for preserving the company's identity and ensuring cohesion among employees. Hiring individuals who align with the company's values can help reinforce its culture, even as the workforce becomes more diverse. If collaboration is a core value of the organization, it's important to hire individuals who prioritize teamwork and communication. Interview questions and assessments that focus on cultural alignment can help identify candidates who will contribute positively to the existing workplace dynamic.

Structuring the team effectively is just as important as hiring the right individuals. As a business grows, the flat, informal structures that often works well in the early stages become less viable. Decisions take longer, communication becomes more complex, and employees may struggle to understand their roles and responsibilities. To address these challenges, entrepreneurs must implement an organizational structure that supports clarity, accountability, and efficiency. This often involves creating clearly defined roles, establishing reporting lines, and introducing management layers as necessary.

While creating a formal structure may feel counterintuitive for founders who value the agility and informality of a small team, it is essential for managing the complexities of a larger organization. If a situation is found in a company that has grown from a team of five to a team of fifty, it may no longer be feasible for the founder to oversee every department directly. Delegating responsibilities to department heads or managers allows for more focused oversight and decision-making. However, it's important to avoid creating unnecessary bureaucracy, which can stifle innovation and slow down the decision-making process. Striking the right balance between structure and flexibility ensures that the organization remains efficient while retaining its ability to adapt quickly to new opportunities or challenges.

Leadership plays a central role in building and structuring a team during growth. As the company expands, the entrepreneur must transition from being a hands-on operator to a strategic leader. This often involves letting go of some responsibilities and trusting the team to take ownership of their respective areas. For many entrepreneurs, this shift can be difficult, as they are accustomed to being deeply involved in every aspect of the business. However, empowering employees with decision-making authority is essential for fostering a sense of ownership and accountability.

Clear communication from leadership is also critical during this phase. Employees need to understand the company's vision, goals, and priorities to align their efforts effectively. Regular updates, town hall meetings, and one-on-one check-ins can help ensure that everyone is on the same page. Furthermore, transparency from leadership builds trust and helps employees feel more connected to the company's mission.

As the team grows, fostering collaboration across departments becomes increasingly important. Silos, where teams or departments operate in isolation from one another, can hinder communication and lead to inefficiencies. When a marketing team does not communicate effectively with the sales team, they may create campaigns that fail to align with the company's sales strategy. Encouraging cross-functional collaboration through regular meetings, shared goals, and integrated workflows can help break down these silos and ensure that all parts of the organization work toward common objectives.

Another consideration when structuring the team is diversity. A diverse workforce brings a range of perspectives, experiences, and ideas that can drive innovation and creativity. During periods of growth, businesses have a unique opportunity to build a team that reflects the diversity of their customer base and the broader community. However, achieving diversity requires intentional effort, from writing inclusive job descriptions to implementing unbiased hiring practices. Beyond the initial hiring process, creating an inclusive work environment where all employees feel valued and supported is essential for retaining diverse talent.

Finally, retaining the right talent is just as important as hiring it. During growth, the pressure and pace of work can lead to burnout if employees are not supported adequately. Offering competitive compensation, professional development opportunities, and a healthy work-life balance can help retain top performers. Recognizing and rewarding contributions, whether through bonuses, promotions, or public acknowledgment, also plays a significant role in keeping employees motivated and engaged.

Hiring and structuring the right team is a multifaceted challenge that requires careful planning and execution. By focusing on strategic hiring, cultural alignment, effective communication, and fostering collaboration, individuals can build a team capable of driving sustainable growth. A well-structured and motivated team not only supports the operational needs of a growing business but also strengthens its culture and positions it for long-term success.

Maintaining quality and consistency during rapid growth is one of the most intricate challenges an entrepreneur can face. As a business expands, the systems, processes, and standards that worked well at a smaller scale may no longer suffice. Growth inevitably introduces complexity, whether through increased customer demands, larger teams, or the diversification of offerings. To preserve the core values and quality that built the business's reputation, entrepreneurs must implement thoughtful strategies and maintain a relentless focus on excellence.

The foundation of maintaining quality during expansion lies in a deep understanding of what defines the business's standards. Every organization has elements that set it apart, be it product craftsmanship, exceptional customer service, or innovative solutions. These differentiators must remain at the forefront of decision-making as the company grows. A bakery known for its artisanal pastries might find it tempting to automate production to meet growing demand. However, doing so without maintaining the handmade touch that customers value could dilute the very quality that drove its success. Understanding and prioritizing these non-negotiable elements ensures that growth does not compromise the company's identity.

One of the greatest risks during rapid expansion is the erosion of attention to detail. When orders flood in, or a new market is entered, it becomes easy to focus on meeting deadlines or increasing output at the expense of precision. To counteract this tendency, businesses must build mechanisms for quality assurance into their processes. This might involve conducting regular audits, implementing rigorous testing protocols, or adopting industry-specific standards. For instance, a software company scaling rapidly should prioritize continuous testing to identify and resolve bugs before they impact users. Investing in these practices upfront saves time, money, and reputational damage in the long run.

Consistency is equally vital as quality. Customers and clients build trust in a brand when they receive reliable, predictable outcomes. During expansion, however, achieving consistency becomes more challenging due to the sheer volume of interactions, products, or services being delivered. Standardization is a powerful tool in overcoming this hurdle. By creating clear guidelines, workflows, and documentation, businesses can ensure that every team member follows the same procedures, regardless of the location or scale of operations. Employee training plays a crucial role in preserving quality during growth. As the workforce expands, new employees may not automatically grasp the standards and values that existing team members uphold. Comprehensive onboarding programs and continuous training initiatives help bridge this gap. New hires should be thoroughly educated about the company's expectations, values, and operational practices. Additionally, ongoing learning opportunities ensure that all employees stay updated on best practices, emerging trends, and technological advancements.

Empowering employees to take ownership of quality is another essential strategy. While leadership plays a crucial role in setting standards, the responsibility for maintaining these standards must extend across the organization. Creating a culture where every team member feels accountable for the company's success fosters a collective commitment to excellence. This might involve recognizing employees who go above and beyond to uphold quality or incorporating quality metrics into performance evaluations. When team members understand the impact of their contributions, they are more likely to prioritize precision and reliability in their work.

Customer feedback is an invaluable resource for maintaining quality and consistency. As the business grows, engaging with customers becomes more challenging, yet their insights remain crucial. Regularly soliciting feedback through surveys, reviews, or direct conversations can help identify areas for improvement and reinforce what the company is doing well. For example, a hotel chain expanding to new locations might use guest feedback to fine-tune its services and address any inconsistencies. Furthermore, demonstrating responsiveness to customer concerns such as implementing changes based on their input fosters loyalty and trust.

Technology can also be a powerful ally in maintaining quality during growth. Automation tools, data analytics, and customer relationship management (CRM) systems streamline operations and provide valuable insights. An e-commerce company can use analytics to track shipping times, order accuracy, and customer satisfaction, enabling it to identify trends and address issues proactively. Automation, when used strategically, allows businesses to handle increased volumes without sacrificing the precision or personal touch that customers expect.

Leadership's role in maintaining quality and consistency cannot be overstated. During growth, leaders set the tone for the organization and serve as guardians of its values. Clear communication from leadership about the importance of quality ensures that it remains a priority at every level. Additionally, leaders must model the behaviors they expect from their teams, such as attention to detail, customer focus, and a commitment to continuous improvement. When employees see leadership prioritizing quality, they are more likely to follow suit.

Growth often brings pressure to cut corners in the name of efficiency or cost savings. However, compromising on quality to save time or resources can have long-term repercussions. Customers who notice a decline in quality may lose trust in the brand and seek alternatives, resulting in lost revenue and damage to the company's reputation. While it is important to manage costs effectively, entrepreneurs must resist the temptation to make short-term compromises that undermine the business's long-term success. Finding the right balance between efficiency and quality requires careful planning, regular monitoring, and a willingness to invest in the resources needed to maintain standards.

Resilience is another critical factor in sustaining quality during rapid growth. Challenges and setbacks are inevitable, whether they arise from supply chain disruptions, employee turnover, or unexpected market shifts. Businesses that can quickly adapt to these challenges without compromising their standards are more likely to succeed. Resilience requires both proactive planning such as developing contingency plans and a mindset that embraces problem-solving and innovation.

Ultimately, maintaining quality and consistency during growth is about preserving the trust and loyalty of customers while meeting the demands of an expanding market. This requires a holistic approach that combines robust processes, empowered employees, and unwavering leadership. By staying true to the values and standards that built the business's success, persons can ensure that their growth journey strengthens rather than dilutes their reputation. The path to sustainable expansion lies in balancing ambition with meticulous attention to detail, allowing businesses to flourish while staying firmly rooted in their commitment to excellence.

Managing the challenges that arise during rapid expansion is as much an art as it is a science, requiring a strategic mindset and an ability to adapt to ever-changing circumstances. Growth often brings with it a range of obstacles that can test an entrepreneur's resilience, decision-making skills, and vision. From managing cash flow to sustaining morale, each challenge presents an opportunity to refine processes, strengthen the organization, and foster a culture capable of thriving in the face of adversity. Addressing these hurdles effectively is critical not only to the success of the business but also to ensuring its longevity and relevance in a competitive marketplace.

One of the most immediate challenges of scaling a business is managing financial resources. Rapid growth often necessitates significant investment in areas such as staffing, technology, infrastructure, and marketing. Balancing these expenditures with the need to maintain healthy cash flow can be a delicate act. For many businesses, the sudden increase in demand can strain existing financial systems, leading to delayed payments, rising operational costs, or insufficient capital for reinvestment. Entrepreneurs must prioritize meticulous financial planning to navigate these challenges effectively. Implementing detailed budgets, forecasting future expenses, and closely monitoring cash flow are essential strategies.

Securing external funding can provide a lifeline during periods of rapid growth, but it comes with its own set of challenges. Entrepreneurs must weigh the advantages and risks of various funding options, from loans and venture capital to equity partnerships. While additional capital can fuel expansion, it may also involve giving up a degree of control or taking on debt. The key is to align funding decisions with the company's long-term goals and growth trajectory. Another challenge during growth is maintaining operational efficiency. As the scale of operations increases, the systems and processes that once worked smoothly may begin to falter. Inefficiencies can manifest in various ways, such as bottlenecks in production, delays in delivery, or miscommunication between departments. Entrepreneurs must take a proactive approach to identifying and addressing these issues. Streamlining workflows, adopting new technologies, and delegating responsibilities can help enhance efficiency.

For instance, a retail business expanding into new markets might implement an advanced inventory management system to ensure products are always in stock without overburdening their supply chain.

In addition to operational challenges, sustaining employee morale during periods of rapid change is another critical consideration. Growth often brings increased workloads, tighter deadlines, and heightened pressure, which can lead to stress and burnout among employees. Fostering a supportive work environment is essential to keeping teams motivated and engaged. This might involve offering flexible work arrangements, providing access to wellness programs, or simply ensuring that employees feel valued and appreciated. Recognizing outstanding performance through bonuses, promotions, or public acknowledgment can go a long way in boosting morale.

Communication becomes increasingly important as the organization grows. In smaller teams, information often flows naturally, with everyone aware of goals, challenges, and successes. However, as the business expands, maintaining this level of transparency and alignment becomes more complex. Entrepreneurs must establish robust communication channels to keep everyone informed and engaged. Regular team meetings, newsletters, and collaborative platforms can help ensure that all employees are aligned with the company's mission and priorities. Doing this and encouraging open dialogue and feedback fosters a sense of inclusion and ensures that employees feel heard.

Customer relationships can also be tested during rapid expansion. While growth often means reaching new markets and serving a larger customer base, it can also lead to a decline in the personal touch that initially endeared customers to the brand. Maintaining a high level of customer satisfaction requires a commitment to understanding and meeting their evolving needs. This might involve investing in customer support teams, implementing feedback mechanisms, or refining the user experience. If your brand or platform is scaling its operations, it might introduce chatbots to handle basic queries while ensuring that complex issues are escalated to trained representatives.

Entrepreneurs must also be prepared to navigate external challenges, such as changes in market conditions, competition, or regulatory environments. Expansion often brings increased scrutiny from regulators, particularly in industries with strict compliance requirements. Staying ahead of these challenges requires a deep understanding of the regulatory landscape and a willingness to adapt quickly. For instance, a financial services company entering new markets might need to navigate varying legal requirements related to data privacy, anti-money laundering, and consumer protection.

Competition is another external factor that can intensify during growth. As a business gains visibility and market share, it may attract the attention of established players or new entrants looking to capitalize on its success. To stay ahead, founders must continually innovate and differentiate their offerings. This could mean introducing new products, improving existing services, or finding creative ways to enhance the customer experience.

Adapting to cultural differences is another challenge that can arise during international expansion. Businesses entering new regions must navigate differences in language, customs, consumer preferences, and business practices. Failing to account for these differences can lead to misunderstandings, missteps, or even a complete failure to gain traction in the new market. Conducting thorough market research, seeking local partnerships, and hiring individuals with cultural expertise can help mitigate these risks. It is advisable that any brand entering a foreign market might need to tailor its marketing campaigns and product offerings to align with local tastes and preferences.

Leadership plays a critical role in overcoming the challenges of growth. Entrepreneurs must demonstrate vision, resilience, and adaptability to guide their organizations through periods of change. This often involves making difficult decisions, such as reallocating resources, pivoting strategies, or even scaling back certain initiatives to focus on core priorities. At the same time, leaders must remain committed to the company's values and mission, ensuring that these principles serve as a compass amid the complexities of expansion.

Building a strong leadership team is equally important. As the business grows, the demands on the entrepreneur's time and energy will inevitably increase. Delegating responsibilities to trusted leaders allows the entrepreneur to focus on high-level strategy while ensuring that day-to-day operations are managed effectively. This might involve hiring experienced executives, promoting them from within, or seeking mentorship and advice from industry experts.

Finally, persons must cultivate a mindset of continuous learning and improvement. Growth is a dynamic process, and the strategies that work at one stage may not be effective at the next. Staying open to new ideas, embracing feedback, and remaining agile in the face of uncertainty are all essential qualities for navigating the challenges of expansion. By approaching these challenges as opportunities for growth and innovation, entrepreneurs can position their businesses for long-term success and sustainability.

In summary, the challenges of growth are multifaceted and require a holistic approach to overcome. By managing financial resources wisely, maintaining operational efficiency, fostering employee engagement, and staying attuned to customer needs, entrepreneurs can navigate the complexities of expansion while preserving the integrity of their businesses. Leadership, adaptability, and a commitment to excellence are the cornerstones of overcoming these hurdles and transforming them into steppingstones for future success.

CHAPTER EIGHT
FAIL FAST, LEARN FASTER

Failure is often seen as a setback, an obstacle that signals the end of a dream. However, for entrepreneurs, failure is more accurately a stepping stone and a necessary part of the journey to success. In the unpredictable world of entrepreneurship, where innovation meets risk, failure serves as both a teacher and a catalyst for growth. Far from being something to fear, it is a fundamental component of building resilience, fostering innovation, and shaping long-term success. To truly understand this, we must explore the role failure plays in entrepreneurship, both globally and closer to home, with stories from far and wide that demonstrate its transformative power.

One of the most iconic examples of failure leading to success comes from Thomas Edison, the inventor of the electric light bulb. Edison is famously quoted as saying, "I have not failed. I've just found 10,000 ways that won't work." His relentless experimentation and willingness to embrace failure were crucial in achieving groundbreaking innovation. For Edison, each failure was not an endpoint but a lesson, a guidepost that brought him closer to his goal. This mindset is vital for entrepreneurs. It reframes failure as a necessary detour on the path to discovery rather than a dead end.

Closer to home, the story of Jason Njoku, the Nigerian entrepreneur and co-founder of iROKOtv, provides a compelling example of how failure can lay the groundwork for eventual success. Before launching iROKOtv, a streaming platform that became known as the "Netflix of Africa," Njoku experienced numerous failed ventures. From a blog advertising company to a student magazine, his early attempts at business were met with setbacks. Yet, each failure taught him invaluable lessons about the market, consumer behavior, and the realities of entrepreneurship. These experiences culminated in the creation of iROKOtv, which capitalized on the growing demand for Nollywood films among the African diaspora. Today, the platform is celebrated as a pioneer in African digital content distribution, proving that failure, when embraced and learned from, can lead to transformative success.

Failure plays a crucial role in fostering innovation. In many cases, the best ideas emerge not from initial success but from the ashes of failed attempts. Consider the story of M-Pesa, the mobile money platform that revolutionized financial transactions in Kenya and beyond. Before becoming a success, M-Pesa's journey involved missteps, including initial resistance from regulators and challenges in understanding user behavior. The early iterations of the platform didn't gain traction as expected, but its developers used these setbacks to refine their approach. By listening to user feedback and adapting their model, they created a system that now empowers millions of people in Africa with access to financial services.

Without these early failures, the team might never have uncovered the insights needed to build such a transformative solution.

In Nigeria, Paystack's journey to becoming a leading fintech company illustrates how failure can drive innovation. The company's founders, Shola Akinlade and Ezra Olubi, faced numerous challenges when trying to establish a payment system tailored to African businesses. Initial attempts to secure funding were met with rejection, and early prototypes of their platform faced technical and operational difficulties. However, instead of being discouraged, they used these experiences to refine their product and pitch. Their persistence paid off, and Paystack grew into a platform that processes millions of transactions across Africa. Its eventual acquisition by Stripe for $200 million underscores how failure coupled with determination and learning can lead to global success.

Failure also shapes better decision-making. When entrepreneurs confront setbacks, they are forced to evaluate their decisions critically, identify what went wrong, and refine their strategies. This iterative process of learning from mistakes fosters a deeper understanding of the market and builds stronger decision-making skills. A classic example is the story of Sir Richard Branson, the founder of Virgin Group. Branson's ventures have not always been successful; Virgin Cola, for instance, was a notable failure. Despite initial enthusiasm, the product struggled to compete with established giants like Coca-Cola and Pepsi. Rather than allowing this failure to define him, Branson used the experience to hone his focus on industries where Virgin could offer unique value, such as music, travel, and telecommunications. This strategic pivot contributed to Virgin's status as a globally recognized brand.

On the African continent, the story of Konga, a Nigerian e-commerce platform, highlights the lessons failure can teach about strategic decision-making. Konga initially aimed to compete with global players like Amazon by adopting a similar model. However, it faced numerous challenges, including infrastructure limitations, logistical difficulties, and intense competition. Despite setbacks, the company adapted by focusing on integrating offline and online retail channels, a strategy more suited to the Nigerian market. This shift, though born out of initial failure, allowed it to survive and evolve in a challenging business environment.

Mentioned numerous times, resilience is another critical outcome of embracing failure. Entrepreneurs who experience setbacks and rise again often emerge stronger, more adaptable, and better equipped to handle future challenges. Aliko Dangote, Africa's richest man, exemplifies this. In the early stages of building his business empire, Dangote faced financial difficulties and operational hurdles. Some of his early investments in manufacturing encountered significant setbacks, including supply chain disruptions and market instability. Yet, his resilience and ability to learn from these challenges enabled him to build one of the most successful conglomerates in Africa, spanning industries such as cement, sugar, and oil.

Similarly, entrepreneurs like Funke Opeke, the founder of MainOne, have shown how resilience can transform failure into opportunity. Opeke returned to Nigeria after a successful career in the United States, determined to address the lack of reliable internet connectivity in West Africa. Her journey was fraught with challenges, including securing funding for her ambitious project of laying a subsea cable. Despite numerous rejections and financial hurdles, Opeke persevered, and MainOne eventually succeeded in transforming internet access across the region. Her story underscores the importance of resilience in overcoming failure and achieving lasting impact.

Globally, the startup ecosystem has embraced the concept of failing fast as a way to accelerate learning and innovation. This philosophy encourages entrepreneurs to experiment, take risks, and view setbacks as opportunities to iterate and improve. Companies like SpaceX, led by Elon Musk, embody this mindset. SpaceX's early rocket launches ended in failure, with explosions and technical malfunctions threatening to derail the company's vision. Yet, each failure was meticulously analyzed, leading to improvements that ultimately resulted in successful launches and groundbreaking achievements, such as reusable rockets. The organization's journey demonstrates that failure is not a sign of defeat but a steppingstone to greater accomplishments.

Honestly, failure is not the enemy of entrepreneurship but an essential element of the journey. It fosters innovation by encouraging experimentation, sharpens decision-making through critical evaluation, and builds resilience by teaching entrepreneurs to persevere in the face of adversity. From the inspiring stories of Nigerian entrepreneurs like Jason Njoku and Funke Opeke to global examples such as Richard Branson and Elon Musk, it is clear that failure, when embraced with the right mindset, can lead to transformative success. Entrepreneurs who understand and accept the role of failure are better equipped to navigate the challenges of building and scaling their businesses, turning setbacks into the foundation for lasting achievement.

A viable aspect of embracing failure as part of success is learning from setbacks. This is the hallmark of successful entrepreneurship, and those who master the ability to extract wisdom from failure set themselves apart in their journey toward building enduring businesses. While failure often feels like a stumbling block, it can instead be a springboard when approached with the right strategies. Founders who methodically analyze their mistakes, refine their approaches, and develop actionable insights are not just surviving; they are actively transforming their setbacks into competitive advantages. This section delves into the art of learning from failure and outlines strategies for turning moments of defeat into steppingstones for progress.

One of the first and most crucial steps in learning from setbacks is embracing a mindset of self-reflection. This involves looking beyond the surface to identify the underlying reasons for the misstep. Entrepreneurs must resist the temptation to attribute failures solely to external factors such as market conditions or competition and instead scrutinize their own decisions, assumptions, and strategies. Self-reflection is a humbling process, but it is also empowering. It equips individuals with a clearer understanding of what went wrong and why. A person who launches a product that fails to gain traction might initially blame weak marketing efforts or customer indifference. However, a deeper analysis might reveal flaws in the product itself, such as a lack of alignment with customer needs or poor timing in entering the market.

A practical tool for self-reflection is conducting a root-cause analysis. This technique, often used in quality management, involves asking a series of "why" questions to drill down to the origin of a problem. For instance, a Nigerian agri-tech startup facing logistics delays might ask: Why are deliveries late? If the answer points to vehicle shortages, the next question could be: Why are there insufficient vehicles? This could lead to an exploration of whether the issue lies in budget allocation, supply chain inefficiencies, or poor forecasting. By systematically uncovering the root causes, entrepreneurs can address the true source of the problem rather than just its symptoms.

Another strategy is leveraging feedback from stakeholders, including employees, customers, and investors. Honestly, constructive feedback is invaluable for gaining perspectives that the entrepreneur might have overlooked. Customers, and information around you, can provide insights into why a product or service failed to resonate with them. In the context of Africa, where diverse consumer preferences and cultural nuances play a significant role in business success, understanding the specific needs and expectations of different demographics is essential. A fashion entrepreneur in Nigeria who struggles to sell a new clothing line might discover through customer surveys that the designs were not culturally appropriate or affordable for the target market. Armed with this feedback, the entrepreneur can pivot to create offerings that better align with consumer preferences.

Listening to employees is equally important, as they are often on the front lines of the business and can provide valuable insights into operational challenges. When your company is experiencing high employee turnover, you might gather feedback through anonymous surveys or one-on-one discussions. This could reveal issues such as a lack of growth opportunities, inadequate compensation, or poor management practices. Addressing these concerns not only strengthens the organization but also fosters a culture of openness and trust, which is critical for navigating future challenges.

Learning from setbacks also requires entrepreneurs to adopt a data-driven approach to decision-making. Emotions often run high in the aftermath of failure, making it tempting to rely on gut feelings or impulsive reactions. However, objective data can provide clarity and guide more informed decisions. Incorporating lessons from setbacks into future strategies is another critical step. Entrepreneurs must view failure as part of an iterative process where each attempt builds upon the last. This approach is particularly evident in the technology sector, where the concept of rapid prototyping is widely embraced. In this methodology, products are launched in their simplest form and refined based on user feedback and performance metrics.

Collaboration and mentorship also play a significant role in extracting value from failure. Entrepreneurs who surround themselves with supportive networks are better equipped to navigate setbacks and gain perspective. Peer learning is another powerful way to glean insights from setbacks. Entrepreneurs who openly share their failures with others foster a culture of transparency and collective growth. In Africa, platforms like the Tony Elumelu Foundation provide opportunities for entrepreneurs to exchange experiences, celebrate successes, and discuss challenges. Such forums encourage honest conversations about failure, allowing participants to learn from one another and develop solutions collaboratively. For example, an entrepreneur in Ghana who struggled to scale a poultry farming business might share lessons about the importance of disease control and feed quality, providing valuable insights to others in similar industries.

Embracing a growth mindset is essential for learning from failure. This mindset, popularized by psychologist Carol Dweck, emphasizes the belief that abilities and intelligence can be developed through effort, learning, and persistence. Entrepreneurs with a growth mindset view setbacks as opportunities to expand their knowledge and skills rather than as indicators of inherent limitations. A person attempting to launch a tech startup might initially struggle with coding or understanding the complexities of venture capital. Instead of being discouraged, they could view these challenges as opportunities to acquire new competencies, whether through online courses, networking, or hands-on practice.

Another critical aspect of learning from failure is maintaining a balance between self-compassion and accountability. Entrepreneurs must be kind to themselves, recognizing that failure is a natural part of the journey, but they must also hold themselves accountable for their actions. This balance prevents the erosion of confidence while fostering a sense of responsibility. When you fail to meet a project deadline due to poor time management, you might acknowledge the mistake, learn from it, and implement tools like project management software to ensure better performance in the future.

Celebrating small wins amid setbacks can also bolster morale and reinforce the lessons learned. Recognizing progress, even in the face of larger failures, provides motivation and reinforces the belief that success is attainable. Let's assume you have a target to scale your operations but have been finding the process incredibly difficult, find solace in the impact you have already made in local communities. By celebrating these achievements, the organization can maintain its focus and draw inspiration to overcome future challenges. Learning from setbacks requires a multifaceted approach that combines self-reflection, feedback, data-driven analysis, resilience, and collaboration. Entrepreneurs who adopt these strategies not only transform failures into valuable lessons but also position themselves for long-term success. By embracing a mindset of continuous learning and improvement, they turn setbacks into opportunities for growth, ultimately shaping a stronger and more innovative entrepreneurial journey. Failure, when approached with the right strategies, becomes not a barrier but a bridge to achieving one's goals.

Transforming setbacks into steppingstones requires more than just recovering from failure but also involves leveraging the lessons learned to innovate, pivot, and build a stronger foundation for success. Entrepreneurs who master this art not only overcome adversity but also position themselves for long-term growth and impact. Across the globe, including Africa and Nigeria, countless stories illustrate how businesses have used setbacks as catalysts for reinvention and innovation. These examples, paired with practical strategies, demonstrate how to turn adversity into opportunity.

A remarkable way setbacks can become steppingstones is by forcing entrepreneurs to pivot toward more promising opportunities. A classic global example is Twitter. The platform we know today began as a podcasting service called Odeo. When Apple launched its podcasting feature on iTunes, Odeo was rendered nearly obsolete. Instead of giving up, the team reimagined their product and created Twitter, which has since become a global social media giant. This story underscores how failure can spark the creativity needed to find a new direction.

In Nigeria, the journey of Flutterwave, one of Africa's leading fintech companies, illustrates a similar resilience and adaptability. During its early days, the startup faced significant challenges in understanding and navigating the complexities of financial systems across different African countries. Initial attempts to streamline cross-border payments were met with resistance from regulators and users unfamiliar with such systems. Rather than being deterred, Flutterwave leveraged these challenges to refine its offerings. By collaborating with banks and local partners, it created a more inclusive payment infrastructure. Today, the company processes billions of dollars in transactions and plays a pivotal role in connecting African businesses to the global economy.

Innovation is often born out of necessity, and failure frequently provides the impetus for such innovation. Take the case of Nigeria's Gokada which is a motorcycle-hailing service that faced a significant setback in 2020 when the Lagos State government banned commercial motorcycles. For a business heavily reliant on this mode of transport, the ban could have spelled the end. However, Gokada turned this challenge into an opportunity to pivot. The company rebranded itself as a logistics and delivery service, leveraging its existing infrastructure to serve the burgeoning e-commerce sector. This strategic shift not only saved the company but also positioned it as a key player in Nigeria's logistics industry.

Time and time again, businesses and entrepreneurs can use a technique to turn setbacks into opportunities and that skill is storytelling. Sharing one's journey, including the failures, can humanize the brand, inspire others, and build a loyal community. Tony Elumelu, the Nigerian entrepreneur and founder of the Tony Elumelu Foundation, often speaks candidly about his early challenges in business. By highlighting his setbacks and the lessons he learned, he has inspired countless African entrepreneurs to persevere in the face of adversity. This openness has also strengthened his personal brand and the credibility of his foundation, which supports entrepreneurship across the continent. Another strategy for transforming failure into opportunity is collaboration. Partnering with others who have complementary strengths can help overcome challenges and create new pathways for growth. A compelling example comes from Andela, the Nigerian-founded tech talent company. When Andela initially launched, it faced difficulties in convincing global tech firms to hire African developers. Instead of retreating, the organization formed partnerships with major companies like Microsoft and Google, leveraging these alliances to validate its value proposition. These collaborations not only helped the company gain credibility but also paved the way for its growth as a leader in talent development.

On a global scale, the story of Airbnb serves as another example of leveraging failure to identify new opportunities. During its early days, the company struggled to gain traction, and its founders even resorted to selling custom cereal boxes to stay afloat. Instead of giving up, they used these challenging times to deeply understand their users' needs, refine their platform, and build a business model that resonated with travelers seeking affordable, unique accommodations. Today, the company is a multibillion-dollar company that has revolutionized the hospitality industry.

A feasible approach to turning setbacks into opportunities is using failure as a moment to reset and refocus on core values. When a business becomes too focused on growth or profitability at the expense of its mission, failure can serve as a wake-up call. For example, in the early 2000s, Ethiopian Airlines faced financial difficulties and operational inefficiencies. Instead of cutting corners to survive, the airline doubled down on its commitment to quality and innovation. By investing in training, modernizing its fleet, and expanding its routes, Ethiopian Airlines emerged stronger and is now one of Africa's most successful and respected airlines.

Founders who successfully transform setbacks into steppingstones also understand the importance of timing. Sometimes, failure occurs because a product or service is introduced to the market too early or too late. Understanding and adapting to market timing can turn a failed venture into a successful one.

Another critical element in turning setbacks into opportunities is fostering a culture of learning within the organization. Businesses that encourage experimentation and view failure as part of the innovation process are better equipped to adapt and grow. In South Africa, Yoco, a fintech company providing payment solutions for small businesses, faced numerous challenges in its early days, including skepticism from potential users. By fostering a culture that embraced feedback and continuous improvement, Yoco was able to refine its product and expand its reach, becoming a trusted partner for small businesses across the continent. Finally, transforming setbacks into steppingstones requires unwavering belief in the vision. Entrepreneurs who remain committed to their purpose, even in the face of repeated failures, often find ways to turn adversity into an advantage.

Setbacks are not the end of the entrepreneurial journey but an integral part of it. By pivoting, innovating, collaborating, and learning from failure, entrepreneurs can transform challenges into opportunities for growth and impact. Stories from Nigeria, Africa, and the world highlight how adversity can become a catalyst for reinvention, proving that failure is not a barrier but a bridge to success. Entrepreneurs who embrace this mindset are not just surviving rather than thriving, building businesses that are stronger, more resilient, and better equipped to create lasting value.

CHAPTER NINE
THE SOCIAL IMPACT OF ENTREPRENEURSHIP: GIVING BACK THROUGH BUSINESS

Entrepreneurship has traditionally been viewed through the lens of financial success, with profit margins and market share serving as the ultimate indicators of achievement. However, the narrative is shifting as modern entrepreneurs increasingly recognize the profound impact their ventures can have beyond economic gains. The concept of success is being redefined, with an emphasis on balancing profitability with purpose. This evolution reflects a growing acknowledgment that businesses have the capacity and arguably the responsibility to address societal challenges while maintaining their viability and growth.

In the past, the primary objective of most enterprises was to maximize returns for shareholders. Founders focused on scaling operations, expanding market reach, and optimizing processes to achieve financial dominance. While these goals remain integral to business, the world has witnessed the emergence of a new paradigm: one that values ethical conduct, social impact, and community well-being alongside financial performance. This transformation is not only a response to societal expectations but also a strategic decision driven by the realization that purpose-driven businesses often outperform those solely motivated by profit.

Balancing profit with purpose begins with understanding that entrepreneurship is deeply interconnected with the society in which it operates. Businesses rely on the support of communities, resources, and ecosystems to thrive. By addressing the challenges faced by these communities whether it be unemployment, inequality, environmental degradation, or access to education, entrepreneurs can create a reciprocal relationship that benefits both their ventures and the people they serve. This approach fosters loyalty, enhances brand reputation, and establishes a legacy that transcends financial achievements.

A compelling example of this shift can be seen in the rise of social enterprises. These businesses prioritize solving societal problems while generating revenue to sustain their operations. For instance, TOMS Shoes revolutionized the concept of giving back with its "One for One" model, where a pair of shoes is donated for every pair purchased. While the company's primary product is footwear, its overarching mission is to improve the lives of underserved populations. This approach not only fulfills a humanitarian purpose but also resonates deeply with consumers, who increasingly seek to support brands that align with their values. Closer to home in Africa, the story of Tony Elumelu and his foundation exemplifies the integration of profit and purpose. Through the Tony Elumelu Foundation, he has championed entrepreneurship as a tool for economic transformation across the continent. By funding and mentoring thousands of aspiring entrepreneurs, he is addressing critical issues such as youth unemployment and poverty while fostering innovation and self-reliance. This initiative underscores how successful entrepreneurs can leverage their resources and influence to create opportunities for others, ultimately contributing to the broader development of society.

Balancing profit with purpose also requires a shift in mindset. Individuals must move beyond the transactional nature of traditional business and adopt a relational approach that values long-term impact over immediate gains. This perspective aligns with the concept of stakeholder capitalism, which advocates addressing the needs of all stakeholders including employees, customers, suppliers, and the environment rather than focusing solely on shareholders. Companies like Patagonia have embraced this philosophy, embedding environmental sustainability into their core operations. By committing to using recycled materials, reducing carbon emissions, and donating profits to environmental causes, Patagonia demonstrates that it is possible to prioritize social good without compromising business success.

In Nigeria, the fintech sector offers numerous examples of enterprises balancing profitability with social impact. Companies like Paystack and Flutterwave are not only enabling seamless financial transactions but also driving financial inclusion for millions of people who previously lacked access to banking services. By addressing systemic challenges such as the exclusion of small businesses from the formal financial system, these startups are fostering economic empowerment and bridging gaps that hinder societal progress. Their success illustrates that aligning business objectives with societal needs can lead to widespread benefits.

Now, the concept of purpose extends beyond philanthropy or corporate social responsibility. It involves embedding social impact into the very fabric of the business model. This requires entrepreneurs to identify areas where their products, services, or operations can directly address societal challenges. Renewable energy companies like M-KOPA in East Africa are tackling the issue of energy poverty by providing affordable solar power solutions to low-income households. By making clean energy accessible, M-KOPA is not only reducing reliance on harmful fossil fuels but also improving the quality of life for thousands of families. This model highlights the potential for businesses to drive systemic change while remaining commercially viable.

The pursuit of purpose is also a strategic advantage in today's business environment. Consumers, particularly younger generations, are increasingly drawn to brands that align with their values. Surveys consistently show that people are willing to pay a premium for products and services from companies that demonstrate ethical behavior and social responsibility. This trend reflects a broader cultural shift where individuals prioritize meaning and impact in their purchasing decisions. For entrepreneurs, this presents an opportunity to differentiate their offerings by emphasizing their commitment to creating positive change.

In the Nigerian context, entrepreneurs like Temie Giwa-Tubosun of LifeBank exemplify the integration of profit and purpose. LifeBank, a health tech company, addresses the critical issue of blood supply shortages by connecting blood banks to hospitals using technology. By improving the efficiency and reliability of blood distribution, the institution saves lives while operating as a sustainable business. Giwa-Tubosun's work illustrates how entrepreneurial ventures can tackle deeply entrenched societal problems with innovative solutions that generate both social and economic value. However, balancing profit with purpose is not without its challenges. Entrepreneurs must navigate the complexities of aligning their mission with financial realities. Striking this balance often requires difficult decisions, such as prioritizing social outcomes over short-term profitability or investing in sustainable practices that may initially increase costs. These challenges necessitate a clear vision, strong leadership, and an unwavering commitment to the broader mission.

Communication is a must have in this dispensation. Entrepreneurs must communicate their purpose effectively to build trust and inspire stakeholders. Transparent and authentic storytelling is essential in conveying the values that drive the business. This involves not only highlighting successes but also acknowledging challenges and setbacks. By sharing their journey, individuals can build credibility and foster deeper connections with their audience. Brands like Apple and Tesla have mastered this art, using compelling narratives to showcase their commitment to innovation and societal impact.

A critical aspect of balancing profit with purpose is measuring and evaluating impact. Entrepreneurs must establish metrics that capture the social, environmental, and economic outcomes of their efforts. This data is invaluable for assessing progress, identifying areas for improvement, and demonstrating accountability to stakeholders. Organizations such as the B Corporation movement have developed frameworks to certify businesses that meet high standards of social and environmental performance. These certifications provide a tangible way for persons to validate their commitment to purpose-driven business.

The redefinition of success in entrepreneurship represents a paradigm shift that aligns economic pursuits with societal needs. Balancing profit with purpose is not only a moral imperative but also a strategic advantage in a world where consumers, employees, and investors increasingly value impact over pure financial gain. By addressing societal challenges, fostering community well-being, and integrating purpose into their operations, entrepreneurs can create a legacy that transcends profit. This approach not only ensures the sustainability of their ventures but also contributes to a more equitable and resilient society. As the stories of TOMS Shoes, Tony Elumelu, LifeBank, and countless others demonstrate, the most successful entrepreneurs are those who recognize that true success lies in the intersection of profitability and purpose.

Entrepreneurship has become a powerful tool for addressing societal challenges by fostering innovation and implementing practical solutions. Businesses today are increasingly expected to go beyond the traditional focus on profit and actively participate in solving pressing issues such as poverty, education, health, and environmental sustainability. This shift is not merely a trend but a profound transformation in how businesses perceive their role in society. Entrepreneurs are at the forefront of this movement, using their creativity, resources, and determination to tackle systemic problems in ways that governments and nonprofits often cannot. Their ability to craft innovative solutions positions them as key players in driving meaningful and sustainable change.

To fully grasp the concept of the tremendous impact this industry is making across the globe, we will examine various areas and practical examples to illustrate the point further. One of the most significant areas where entrepreneurs are making an impact is poverty alleviation. Across the globe, innovative business models are providing pathways for individuals and communities to break free from the cycle of poverty. In Africa, this is particularly evident in the rise of businesses focused on financial inclusion. Mobile money platforms such as M-Pesa in Kenya have revolutionized access to financial services for millions of unbanked individuals. By enabling users to send, receive, and save money using their mobile phones, the business has not only improved financial security but also empowered small business owners to expand their operations. This model has inspired similar initiatives across the continent, demonstrating the transformative potential of technology-driven solutions.

In Nigeria, businesses like Farmcrowdy have addressed poverty by targeting the agricultural sector, which employs a significant portion of the population. The organization connects small-scale farmers with investors who provide funding for agricultural projects. In return, the investors receive a share of the profits from the harvest. This innovative approach not only supports farmers with the resources they need to increase productivity but also creates a sustainable investment opportunity for individuals looking to support local economies. By bridging the gap between farmers and capital, the company exemplifies how entrepreneurship can directly address poverty while fostering economic growth.

Education is another domain where entrepreneurs are driving impactful solutions. The lack of access to quality education remains a critical challenge in many developing regions, including parts of Africa. Entrepreneurs are tackling this issue by leveraging technology to make education more accessible and affordable. For example, Andela, a company with roots in Nigeria, identifies and trains talented individuals in software development, connecting them with global employment opportunities. By addressing the skills gap and creating pathways for high-paying jobs in the tech industry, the institution is not only transforming individual lives but also contributing to the broader goal of economic empowerment.

Health care is another pressing area where entrepreneurial innovation is making a difference. In regions with limited access to medical resources, entrepreneurs are developing solutions that prioritize affordability and efficiency. One standout example is LifeBank in Nigeria, a health tech company dedicated to improving the distribution of essential medical supplies, such as blood and oxygen. By using digital platforms and data-driven logistics, LifeBank ensures that hospitals receive critical supplies promptly, potentially saving thousands of lives. This model illustrates how entrepreneurial ventures can address systemic health challenges while operating financially sustainable businesses.

On a global scale, businesses are also addressing environmental challenges, recognizing the urgency of mitigating climate change and preserving natural resources. Renewable energy companies, for instance, are creating innovative solutions to reduce reliance on fossil fuels. In Africa, companies like M-KOPA have pioneered affordable solar energy solutions for households that lack access to electricity. By providing pay-as-you-go solar kits, M-KOPA not only addresses energy poverty but also reduces carbon emissions, offering a sustainable alternative to traditional energy sources. This approach highlights the potential for entrepreneurs to align environmental conservation with business growth.

In the realm of clean water access, businesses like Water Access Rwanda are providing innovative solutions to communities in need. By installing decentralized water purification systems, this venture ensures that underserved populations have access to clean and safe drinking water. This business model not only addresses a fundamental human right but also generates revenue to sustain operations, demonstrating that social impact and profitability are not mutually exclusive.

Entrepreneurs are also tackling societal challenges through partnerships and collaboration. Many complex issues, such as gender inequality and urbanization, require multi-stakeholder approaches to drive significant change. Businesses are increasingly working alongside governments, nonprofit organizations, and local communities to amplify their impact. In Nigeria, She Leads Africa is a platform that supports female entrepreneurs by providing resources, mentorship, and access to funding. By fostering a network of women leaders, She Leads Africa is addressing gender disparities while promoting economic development. This collaborative model underscores the importance of partnerships in achieving meaningful and lasting outcomes.

One of the defining features of entrepreneurial solutions to societal challenges is their scalability. Founders design their ventures to grow and replicate, ensuring that their impact extends beyond the initial community or region they serve. For example, the success of mobile money platforms in Africa has inspired similar initiatives in Asia and Latin America, highlighting the global applicability of such solutions. Similarly, renewable energy companies that begin in underserved areas often expand to urban markets, proving that sustainable solutions can be both impactful and profitable on a scale.

The use of technology is another key driver of innovative solutions. Entrepreneurs are leveraging advancements in artificial intelligence, blockchain, and data analytics to address complex issues more effectively. In the agricultural sector, precision farming technologies are helping farmers optimize yields while minimizing environmental impact. In education, online learning platforms break down geographical barriers and enabling students to access quality resources from anywhere in the world. These technological innovations not only enhance efficiency but also create opportunities for greater inclusion and accessibility.

In addition to creating innovative solutions, entrepreneurs are also shaping the narrative around societal challenges. By highlighting these issues through their work, they raise awareness and inspire others to take action. This influence extends beyond their immediate ventures, as their stories often serve as catalysts for broader movements. For example, the founders of companies like TOMS Shoes and Warby Parker have used their platforms to advocate for social causes, encouraging consumers and businesses alike to prioritize impact over profit. Their leadership demonstrates the role entrepreneurs can play in driving cultural change.

Despite the remarkable progress being made, addressing societal challenges through entrepreneurship comes with its own set of obstacles. Entrepreneurs often face resistance from entrenched systems or skepticism about the viability of socially oriented business models. Funding can also be a significant hurdle, as impact-driven ventures may not align with traditional investment criteria. However, the rise of impact investing and social venture funds is helping to bridge this gap, providing entrepreneurs with the resources they need to scale their solutions.

There is no doubt that entrepreneurship holds immense potential to address societal challenges by creating innovative, scalable, and sustainable solutions. From poverty alleviation and education to health care and environmental conservation, individuals are demonstrating that businesses can be powerful agents of change. By leveraging technology, fostering collaboration, and prioritizing impact, they are transforming lives and reshaping communities. The examples from Africa, such as Farmcrowdy, LifeBank, and M-KOPA, illustrate how these solutions are not limited by geography but resonate with the universal need for progress and equity. As more entrepreneurs embrace the challenge of solving societal issues, the world moves closer to achieving a future where business success is measured not just by financial gains but by the positive changes it brings to humanity.

The business industry is uniquely positioned to empower communities, foster local development, and address the systemic inequities that limit opportunities for marginalized groups. Beyond profit-making, businesses have the capacity to drive transformative change by creating pathways to economic participation, providing essential services, and cultivating environments where underserved populations can thrive. This role as a community catalyst not only elevates the lives of individuals but also strengthens the social fabric, contributing to sustainable development and long-term stability.

Empowering communities begins with recognizing that economic inequality and social exclusion are barriers that stifle growth and potential. Entrepreneurs, through their ventures, have the ability to bridge these gaps by designing inclusive business models that create employment, build skills, and generate income for those often left behind. In many parts of Africa and other developing regions, small and medium-sized enterprises (SMEs) serve as lifelines for communities, addressing local challenges and stimulating economic activity where larger corporations often fail to reach.

In Nigeria, for instance, several entrepreneurs are making significant strides in empowering marginalized groups. One notable example is the work of Achenyo Idachaba, founder of Mitimeth, a company that transforms invasive aquatic weeds into eco-friendly, handcrafted products. By employing local artisans, particularly women, the company not only addresses environmental issues but also creates economic opportunities for individuals in rural areas. This initiative demonstrates how entrepreneurship can simultaneously tackle multiple challenges from environmental degradation, unemployment, and gender inequality through innovative solutions.

Another powerful example from Africa is Ethiopia's shoe company SoleRebels. Founded by Bethlehem Tilahun Alemu, SoleRebels employs traditional craftsmanship to create high-quality footwear for global markets. The company hires artisans from disadvantaged communities, providing them with stable incomes and access to international markets. This model not only empowers individuals by preserving cultural heritage but also challenges the notion that businesses in developing regions cannot compete on a global scale. SoleRebels has proven that local talent, when given the right opportunities, can achieve remarkable success while uplifting entire communities.

Education and skill development are central to community empowerment, and entrepreneurs play a pivotal role in providing these opportunities. In many underserved areas, access to quality education and vocational training is limited, perpetuating cycles of poverty. Social entrepreneurs are stepping in to fill these gaps by offering programs that equip individuals with the skills needed to participate in the modern economy. Nigeria's Babban Gona, an agricultural franchise that trains and supports smallholder farmers, enabling them to increase productivity and income. By providing access to quality inputs, training, and credit, the organization transforms subsistence farmers into entrepreneurs, fostering economic empowerment at the grassroots level.

Moreover, businesses can empower communities by supporting local supply chains and fostering entrepreneurship among small vendors and producers. In doing so, they create ripple effects that benefit entire ecosystems. For example, breweries in East Africa, such as those operated by Uganda Breweries Limited, have made a conscious effort to source ingredients from local farmers. This approach not only reduces costs and ensures a steady supply of raw materials but also provides farmers with consistent income and incentives to improve their agricultural practices.

The result is a mutually beneficial relationship that strengthens both the business and the surrounding community.

Individuals can also address systemic gender inequalities by empowering women through targeted initiatives. Women, particularly in developing regions, often face disproportionate barriers to economic participation, including limited access to capital, education, and employment opportunities. Businesses that prioritize gender inclusivity have the potential to transform these dynamics. In Kenya, the company Savanna Circuit provides solar-powered milk chillers to smallholder dairy farmers, many of whom are women. This innovation reduces milk spoilage, increases income, and improves livelihoods, empowering women to take charge of their economic futures. Such initiatives highlight how entrepreneurship can dismantle structural barriers and create opportunities for historically marginalized groups. Apart from addressing gender disparities, entrepreneurship can promote youth empowerment by providing avenues for young people to gain skills, employment, and entrepreneurial experience. Youth unemployment is a pressing issue in many parts of the world, particularly in Africa, where a growing population of young people faces limited job prospects.

The impact of entrepreneurship on communities extends beyond direct economic benefits. Businesses also play a critical role in improving access to essential services such as health care, clean water, and housing. Social enterprises are uniquely equipped to address these needs by designing cost-effective, scalable solutions that reach underserved populations. In South

Africa, the company Zoona provides mobile financial services to communities without access to traditional banking. By offering a secure platform for money transfers, Zoona enables individuals to send and receive funds, supporting financial inclusion and fostering resilience in times of crisis.

Furthermore, entrepreneurial ventures contribute to community empowerment by fostering a sense of ownership and pride among local populations. When businesses are rooted in the communities they serve, they cultivate a sense of shared purpose and collective progress. This connection is evident in cooperatives, where members pool resources and share profits to achieve common goals. In Rwanda, coffee cooperatives have empowered farmers by giving them greater control over pricing, quality, and market access. These cooperatives not only improve incomes but also strengthen social bonds and build resilience against external shocks.

A compelling aspect as a tool for community empowerment is its scalability and adaptability. Unlike traditional aid programs, which are often constrained by funding cycles and bureaucratic processes, entrepreneurial solutions are driven by market forces that encourage efficiency, innovation, and growth. Businesses that succeed in one community can replicate their models in others, amplifying their impact and creating a network of empowered individuals and communities. The success of Grameen Bank in Bangladesh has inspired similar microfinance initiatives around the world, providing millions of people with access to credit and opportunities to escape poverty.

In the midst of these successes, empowering communities through entrepreneurship is not without its challenges. Founders often face resistance from entrenched systems, cultural norms, or power structures that perpetuate inequality. In addition, achieving impact at scale requires significant resources, strategic partnerships, and sustained commitment. Addressing these challenges requires a holistic approach that combines business acumen with social consciousness. People must be willing to engage with stakeholders, adapt to local contexts, and continuously refine their strategies to meet evolving needs.

Moreover, the pursuit of community empowerment must be balanced with the financial sustainability of the business. While the desire to make a difference is a powerful motivator, businesses must remain profitable to ensure their longevity and ability to scale. This balance can be achieved by adopting hybrid models that blend social and economic goals. Many social enterprises use a tiered pricing system, where higher-income customers subsidize services for lower-income populations. This approach ensures that the business remains viable while maximizing its impact on underserved communities.

This career path is a powerful force for community empowerment, creating opportunities for marginalized groups, fostering local development, and addressing systemic inequities. Through innovative business models, skill development programs, and inclusive practices, entrepreneurs are driving transformative change that extends far beyond profit. The examples of Mitimeth, SoleRebels, Babban Gona, and countless others demonstrate the potential of businesses to uplift individuals and communities, building a foundation for sustainable growth and resilience. By prioritizing empowerment alongside economic success, entrepreneurs are not only transforming lives but also contributing to a more equitable and inclusive world. As this movement gains momentum, it serves as a testament to the enduring power of entrepreneurship.

CHAPTER TEN
LEGACY AND LONGEVITY

Building a sustainable business model is the cornerstone of establishing a venture that can endure the test of time. While the allure of quick gains may tempt entrepreneurs to prioritize short-term success, creating a business that lasts demands a deeper, more deliberate approach. It involves crafting a model that adapts to market fluctuations, aligns with customer needs, and sustains financial health while fostering innovation and resilience. This intricate balancing act requires a robust understanding of core principles, a commitment to continuous improvement, and the foresight to anticipate challenges.

At the heart of a sustainable business model lies the ability to deliver consistent value to customers. Businesses that endure often do so because they solve a fundamental problem or fulfill a persistent need in ways that competitors cannot easily replicate. Identifying and deeply understanding this value proposition is essential. It forms the foundation upon which other elements of the business are built.

A customer-centric approach is integral to sustaining a business over the long term. This involves not only understanding the needs and preferences of your target audience but also evolving alongside them as those needs change. Companies that proactively gather feedback and adapt their offerings are better positioned to maintain relevance. MTN Group, a telecommunications giant operating across Africa, continuously invests in infrastructure and technological innovation to enhance service quality. This commitment to customer satisfaction has enabled the company to retain its competitive edge in a rapidly evolving industry. Operational efficiency is another crucial pillar of sustainability. Managing resources effectively, optimizing processes, and reducing waste contribute not only to profitability but also to resilience during economic downturns. Businesses that embrace lean principles and invest in scalable systems are better equipped to handle growth and external shocks.

Financial health and stability are fundamental to the longevity of any business. Entrepreneurs must adopt sound financial planning practices, including prudent budgeting, diversification of revenue streams, and reinvestment of profits. Maintaining a healthy cash flow ensures that the business can weather unexpected challenges and capitalize on growth opportunities. Dangote Group's strategy of reinvesting profits into diversified ventures, such as agriculture and oil refining, exemplifies how long-term financial planning can reinforce a company's stability and expand its impact.

Innovation is a key driver of sustainability, particularly in industries characterized by rapid change. Businesses that cultivate a culture of innovation are better equipped to adapt to shifts in consumer behavior, technological advancements, and market dynamics. This requires creating an environment where experimentation is encouraged, and failure is viewed as a learning opportunity. Globally, companies like Apple have thrived by consistently introducing groundbreaking products that redefine markets. In Africa, Jumia, often referred to as the "Amazon of Africa," has adapted its business model to address local challenges, such as limited infrastructure, by investing in logistics and payment systems tailored to the continent's unique needs.

Collaboration and partnerships also play a vital role in sustaining a business over time. By forging strategic alliances, companies can access new markets, share resources, and pool expertise to tackle challenges more effectively. Partnerships can also enhance credibility and brand recognition. Adapting to market changes is a non-negotiable aspect of building a lasting business. Entrepreneurs must stay attuned to industry trends, regulatory developments, and economic shifts that could impact their operations. This requires a commitment to continuous learning and agility. Companies like Interswitch, a Nigerian digital payment solutions provider, have thrived by anticipating the growing demand for cashless transactions and innovating accordingly. By staying ahead of the curve, businesses can position themselves as leaders rather than followers in their respective industries.

The importance of ethical practices and social responsibility cannot be overstated in the context of sustainability. Consumers and investors increasingly favor businesses that demonstrate a commitment to environmental, social, and governance (ESG) principles. Integrating ethical considerations into business operations not only enhances reputation but also fosters trust among stakeholders. African Clean Energy, a social enterprise, combines sustainable practices with impactful solutions by providing clean cooking technology to underserved communities, thereby addressing both environmental and social challenges.

Sustainability also hinges on a business's ability to manage risks effectively. This involves identifying potential threats, assessing their impact, and implementing strategies to mitigate them. Whether it's economic downturns, supply chain disruptions, or technological obsolescence, businesses that prepare for contingencies are better positioned to navigate uncertainties. Diversification is a common risk management strategy, as evidenced by companies like Nestlé, which operate in multiple product categories and markets to reduce dependence on any single revenue stream.

Leadership plays a pivotal role in fostering sustainability. Visionary leaders who prioritize long-term goals over short-term gains set the tone for their organizations. They inspire teams, make strategic decisions, and instill a sense of purpose that transcends profit. In Africa, entrepreneurs like Strive Masiyiwa, founder of Econet Group, have demonstrated the impact of values-driven leadership in building businesses that last. Masiyiwa's emphasis on innovation, integrity, and social impact has not only ensured Econet's growth but also cemented its legacy as a force for good.

While the principles of sustainability are universal, their application often requires customization to local contexts. Entrepreneurs operating in emerging markets must navigate unique challenges such as infrastructure deficits, regulatory hurdles, and limited access to capital. However, these challenges can also present opportunities for innovation and differentiation. By leveraging local knowledge and resources, businesses can create solutions that are both impactful and scalable.

Education and skill development are critical components of a sustainable business model. Investing in employee training and development not only enhances productivity but also fosters loyalty and reduces turnover. Businesses that prioritize learning create a culture of continuous improvement, which is essential for long-term success. Ultimately, building a sustainable business model is a multifaceted endeavor that requires a clear vision, meticulous planning, and unwavering commitment. It demands a balance between adaptability and consistency, innovation and tradition, growth and responsibility. By focusing on delivering value, optimizing operations, and fostering resilience, entrepreneurs can create businesses that not only endure but also thrive in the face of change. This journey is not without its challenges, but the rewards both financial and societal are well worth the effort. A business built on sustainable principles stands as a testament to its founder's foresight, integrity, and dedication, leaving a legacy that resonates for generations to come.

Establishing a resilient organizational culture is one of the most profound yet intangible assets a business can cultivate. A robust culture acts as a guiding compass, influencing decisions, uniting employees, and fostering an environment where individuals and teams thrive. While profitability and market presence are critical for a business's survival, it is the deeply ingrained values, practices, and attitudes that ensure longevity. A resilient culture does more than weather storms and it transforms challenges into opportunities and sustains a business across generations.

The essence of organizational culture lies in its ability to articulate shared values and inspire collective purpose. It defines how employees interact, make decisions, and approach their work. A thriving culture emphasizes not just what is achieved but how it is accomplished. For instance, First Bank of Nigeria, one of Africa's oldest financial institutions, has endured for over a century partly due to its strong focus on customer-centricity and ethical banking practices. By prioritizing trust and excellence, the institution has consistently aligned its internal operations with the expectations of its customers and stakeholders.

Resilience in culture emerges from adaptability and alignment. The ability to evolve while remaining anchored to core principles is crucial. Organizations must be flexible enough to respond to external changes without losing sight of their foundational identity. This duality is evident in the history of Coca-Cola, a company that has managed to remain a global leader in the beverage industry for over a century. By continually reinventing its marketing strategies and expanding its product portfolio to meet changing consumer tastes, Coca-Cola maintains relevance while preserving its brand legacy.

Employee engagement is another cornerstone of a resilient organizational culture. When employees feel valued, empowered, and aligned with the company's mission, they are more likely to contribute their best efforts. This sense of belonging fosters loyalty and reduces turnover, which is vital for continuity. Google, for example, invests heavily in creating an inclusive, innovative workplace where employees are encouraged to take ownership of projects and think creatively. The result is a culture that not only attracts top talent but also retains it, fueling the company's sustained growth.

Communication is a critical factor in cultivating resilience. Transparent, open communication channels ensure that employees at all levels feel heard and informed. This builds trust and reduces misunderstandings, especially during periods of change or crisis. Inclusivity and diversity are essential components of a culture that endures. Organizations that embrace varied perspectives are better equipped to innovate, solve problems, and navigate complex environments. A diverse workforce reflects the broader community the business serves, fostering a sense of connection and relevance. MTN Group, with operations spanning multiple countries in Africa, has embedded inclusivity into its operations by embracing cultural and regional differences. This strategy has enabled

MTN to build strong relationships with local communities, enhancing its brand and resilience. Celebrating successes and recognizing contributions is another way to reinforce a positive culture. Acknowledging achievements, whether big or small, boosts morale and motivates teams to aim higher. Recognition also creates a sense of continuity, as employees see how their efforts contribute to the organization's overarching goals. Companies like Unilever have institutionalized reward systems that celebrate innovation, collaboration, and impact, ensuring that employees feel appreciated and aligned with the company's mission.

Crisis management is another dimension where resilient cultures shine. Organizations with a strong cultural foundation are better equipped to navigate crises because they possess a shared understanding of priorities and a collective ability to adapt. When the COVID-19 pandemic disrupted global business operations, many companies relied on their culture to guide decision-making. Those with flexible work practices and a commitment to employee well-being, such as Microsoft, were able to pivot effectively, maintaining productivity while safeguarding their workforce.

Building a resilient culture is not a one-time effort; it requires ongoing commitment and reinforcement. Rituals, traditions, and symbols play an important role in embedding cultural values into the daily lives of employees. These elements serve as reminders of what the organization stands for and why its mission matters. Companies like Patagonia, known for its environmental activism, use storytelling and employee engagement activities to reinforce their culture of sustainability. This approach not only aligns employees with the company's mission but also inspires them to advocate for the brand's values externally.

Organizational culture is also deeply influenced by external factors, such as market trends, societal expectations, and technological advancements. As these factors evolve, businesses must strike a delicate balance between preserving their core identity and adapting to new realities. The ability to anticipate and respond to these changes is a hallmark of resilience. For instance, banks in Nigeria have increasingly adopted digital platforms to meet the growing demand for online services, ensuring that they remain relevant in a technology-driven world.

Resilient cultures prioritize the well-being of employees, recognizing that people are the backbone of any business. Companies that invest in mental health resources, work-life balance, and employee support programs create environments where individuals feel cared for and motivated. Access Bank in Nigeria has implemented policies that promote gender equality and work-life harmony, reinforcing its commitment to a supportive and inclusive workplace. Leadership succession is another critical factor in sustaining a resilient culture. Planning for leadership transitions ensures that the organization's values and vision endure even as individuals change. By grooming future leaders from within, businesses can maintain cultural continuity while benefiting from fresh perspectives.

This organizational culture is a powerful asset that extends beyond the confines of the business itself. It becomes a source of identity, pride, and purpose for everyone involved, from employees to customers to communities. By fostering shared values, encouraging adaptability, and prioritizing well-being, organizations can build cultures that not only withstand adversity but also propel them toward enduring success. Through intentionality, persistence, and a focus on people, resilient cultures become the bedrock of businesses that last for decades, leaving a legacy that resonates long after their founders have moved on.

Establishing a legacy in business is a task that transcends the immediate goal of profitability, aiming instead at long-term relevance and impact. Legacy is about crafting an enduring influence, one that outlasts the founder and becomes a testament to the values, principles, and contributions of the enterprise. To build such a legacy, businesses must embrace forward-thinking strategies, ensure intergenerational relevance, and engage with their stakeholders in meaningful ways. Planning for the future while learning from the past ensures that a business is not only successful but also significant over time.

One critical aspect of creating a legacy is identifying a purpose that resonates deeply with society. A mission that goes beyond financial success provides a business with a reason to endure. Organizations that tie their objectives to societal challenges often find that their impact becomes intertwined with their legacy.

A purpose-driven business aligns its activities with its core values, which act as a compass for decision-making and a source of stability. Values such as integrity, innovation, and inclusivity provide a framework that guides the organization through changing market dynamics and unforeseen challenges. When businesses consistently act in accordance with these principles, they build trust and loyalty among stakeholders, which is crucial for longevity. To sustain a legacy, a business must also maintain adaptability. The world is evolving, and businesses that fail to adjust to technological, social, and economic shifts risk becoming obsolete. Adaptability involves a willingness to reassess traditional practices, embrace innovation, and anticipate future trends. Companies like General Electric (GE) demonstrate this principle through their long history of transformation. Founded in 1892, GE has continuously evolved, transitioning from lightbulbs to industrial equipment to renewable energy solutions, ensuring its relevance across multiple eras.

Technological innovation is often a linchpin in maintaining adaptability. The pillar of legacy-building is intergenerational planning. Founders and current leaders must consider how their business will transition to future stewards. Succession planning ensures that leadership changes do not disrupt the organization's mission or erode its culture. Businesses that fail to plan for leadership transitions risk instability and fragmentation, which can diminish their legacy. Family-owned businesses in Africa, such as Nigeria's BUA Group, have successfully incorporated succession planning into their operations. By preparing the next generation of leaders and involving them early in decision-making, these companies preserve their ethos while fostering innovation.

Intergenerational planning is not limited to leadership succession; it also involves preparing the organization itself for long-term sustainability. This includes diversifying revenue streams, expanding into new markets, and investing in research and development.

Stakeholder engagement plays a crucial role in cementing a business's legacy. Engaging with employees, customers, communities, and partners fosters goodwill and strengthens the business's reputation. Open and honest communication with stakeholders ensures alignment between the organization's objectives and the expectations of those it serves. South Africa's Woolworths has built a legacy as a socially responsible retailer by committing to sustainable practices, such as ethical sourcing and environmental conservation. Its transparent engagement with customers and suppliers has solidified its reputation as a company that values more than just profits.

Sustainability is another critical factor in building a business that lasts. A focus on environmental, social, and governance (ESG) factors ensures that the business operates responsibly, minimizing its negative impact while maximizing positive contributions. Businesses that incorporate sustainability into their operations are more likely to attract and retain customers, employees, and investors who value ethical practices. Unilever's "Sustainable Living Plan" is a global example of how a commitment to sustainability can enhance a company's legacy. By integrating sustainable sourcing, waste reduction, and community development into its business model, Unilever has ensured both profitability and positive societal impact.

In Africa, the importance of sustainability is particularly pronounced due to the continent's unique challenges and opportunities. Community engagement is another cornerstone of legacy-building. Businesses that actively contribute to the communities they operate in create lasting bonds and a sense of mutual growth. By investing in education, healthcare, and infrastructure, businesses can make a tangible difference while earning the trust and loyalty of their stakeholders. Philanthropy is a powerful tool for legacy-building, but it must be approached strategically. While donations and sponsorships can provide immediate benefits, long-term impact requires sustained involvement and alignment with the company's mission.

Innovation and creativity are also indispensable in creating a lasting legacy. Businesses that push boundaries and challenge the status quo not only differentiate themselves but also set benchmarks for their industries. Apple's commitment to design and user experience has made it an iconic brand that resonates across generations.

It is not enough to focus solely on financial metrics; businesses must also consider their cultural, social, and environmental contributions. A legacy is created through consistent actions, meaningful engagement, and an unwavering commitment to values. By embracing these principles, entrepreneurs can ensure that their businesses not only succeed in the present but also leave an indelible mark on the future.

Creating a sustainable business model is more than just a strategic maneuver; it is about ensuring the long-term success of a venture by maintaining its relevance in a constantly evolving market. In today's business environment, where unpredictability and disruption are common, establishing a robust and sustainable model is crucial for companies aiming to thrive for decades, if not centuries. A sustainable model enables businesses to weather challenges, adapt to changes, and continue growing. It also allows businesses to contribute to societal development and environmental protection while pursuing profitability.

The first element of a sustainable business model is a strong foundational framework that includes a clearly defined mission and vision. A business purpose provides direction and ensures that everyone within the organization understands the long-term goals. It acts as a compass in decision-making, guiding the business through difficult times. For instance, the mission statement of Tesla— "to accelerate the world's transition to sustainable energy"—is not just a statement but a guiding principle. It shapes Tesla's decisions, from producing electric vehicles to developing energy storage solutions. This mission has been instrumental in positioning Tesla as an innovative leader while being aligned with broader environmental goals.

For businesses to truly thrive in the long term, their sustainability should not be limited to financial viability but must encompass social and environmental dimensions as well. This concept is often referred to as the triple bottom line: people, planet, and profit. Businesses that adopt this holistic approach tend to build deeper relationships with their stakeholders and reduce the negative impact of their operations.

Customer centricity is another essential pillar of a sustainable business model. Understanding customer needs, preferences, and pain points enables businesses to deliver value that resonates with their target audience. As customer expectations evolve, businesses must continually adapt their products and services to meet these changing needs. Companies that excel at customer service and focus on delivering an exceptional experience often find themselves enjoying high levels of loyalty, which is vital for longevity.

In Nigeria, companies like GTBank have built their legacy by focusing on customer experience. GTBank was one of the first Nigerian banks to provide seamless digital banking services, such as internet banking and mobile apps, making banking more accessible for customers. The bank's relentless focus on customer needs, coupled with a robust digital transformation strategy, has helped it maintain a strong market position. By continually improving its offerings and being in tune with customer demands, GTBank has ensured its longevity and relevance in an increasingly competitive sector.

Building a culture of continuous learning and development is also crucial for long-term business success. In today's fast-paced world, businesses must stay ahead of trends and equip their employees with the necessary skills to keep up with industry advancements. Businesses that prioritize employee development and invest in training programs are more likely to innovate, adapt to changes, and remain competitive.

Companies like Microsoft and Google have made continuous learning a core part of their culture. They offer a range of professional development programs and training opportunities to ensure that their employees are always learning and evolving. Securing long-term success requires strong leadership. Leaders play a pivotal role in creating and maintaining a sustainable business model. They must be visionaries who are not only focused on short-term goals but also on ensuring that the company remains relevant and resilient in the long run. Good leadership involves making tough decisions, creating a culture of innovation, and ensuring that the business operates ethically and sustainably.

Successful business owners understand that the journey is long, and they are committed to the sustained growth of their companies over time. This means making strategic investments, building strong relationships with customers and partners, and continuously refining business practices to ensure that they remain relevant in a changing world. Building a business that lasts requires a multifaceted approach. It requires a commitment to sustainability, ethical leadership, innovation, long-term planning, and a focus on community development. Entrepreneurs who are able to balance these elements will not only create successful businesses but also leave behind a meaningful legacy. A legacy that is defined not just by financial success, but by the positive impact a company has on its employees, customers, communities, and the world at large. It is a legacy that continues to grow and thrive, long after the entrepreneurs who started the company are gone. By focusing on creating value beyond profit and considering the long-term societal and environmental impact of their actions, entrepreneurs can build businesses that last for generations, leaving an enduring mark on the world.

CHAPTER ELEVEN
UNDERSTANDING LEGAL AND COMPLIANCE ESSENTIALS

Starting a business is an exciting venture filled with opportunities, but laying a solid legal foundation is critical to its long-term success. Entrepreneurs often focus on their vision, market strategies, and product offerings, but neglecting the legal aspects can lead to significant challenges down the line. Establishing your business legally involves understanding and navigating the regulatory frameworks that govern business operations in your region, ensuring compliance with laws, and protecting your interests. This is particularly important in countries like Nigeria, where the regulatory environment presents unique challenges and opportunities, but the principles extend universally, as these fundamentals are applicable across diverse jurisdictions.

To get started in the process of establishing a business is determining its legal structure. The structure you choose not only defines your legal obligations but also impacts your tax responsibilities, ability to raise funds, and personal liability. For instance, in Nigeria, entrepreneurs can register their businesses as sole proprietorships, partnerships, or limited liability companies. A sole proprietorship is the simplest and most common structure, especially for small businesses and startups. It allows the entrepreneur to maintain complete control while minimizing administrative complexities. However, the downside is that the owner assumes unlimited liability, meaning personal assets are at risk if the business incurs debts or legal claims.

On the other hand, partnerships offer a shared approach to business management and resources. This structure can be beneficial when multiple individuals bring complementary skills and resources to the venture. However, the terms of the partnership need to be clearly outlined in a partnership agreement to prevent future disputes. Issues such as profit-sharing, decision-making, and responsibilities must be detailed to avoid ambiguity. Beyond Nigeria, many jurisdictions encourage partnerships with frameworks that define limited partnerships, where some partners have limited liability while others take on full responsibility for the business.

For entrepreneurs seeking to limit personal liability and facilitate access to funding, forming a limited liability company (LLC) is often the best choice. In Nigeria, the Corporate Affairs Commission (CAC) oversees the registration of LLCs, which provides legal recognition and separates the business's assets and liabilities from the owners. The process involves selecting a unique name, submitting required documentation, and paying registration fees. LLCs offer flexibility in management and ownership structures while providing a shield of liability protection. Globally, similar structures exist, such as private limited companies in the United Kingdom or limited liability corporations in the United States, each tailored to their local regulatory systems.

Once the business structure is chosen, registration becomes the next critical step. In Nigeria, registering with the CAC is mandatory for legal recognition. This process ensures the business operates within the law, grants it the right to trade, and protects its name from being used by others. Registration also allows the business to open corporate bank accounts, which are essential for financial management. Similarly, in other countries, registering a business is a fundamental requirement. For instance, in the United States, businesses must register with federal and state agencies, while in India, registration with the Ministry of Corporate Affairs is necessary. Regardless of location, registration ensures compliance with local laws and provides a foundation for growth.

Beyond registration, founders must obtain the necessary licenses and permits to operate legally. The type of license required depends on the nature of the business and its location. In Nigeria, industries like food production, healthcare, and telecommunications are subject to stringent licensing requirements. For example, food businesses must comply with regulations set by the National Agency for Food and Drug Administration and Control (NAFDAC), ensuring product safety and quality. Similarly, financial institutions must obtain licenses from the Central Bank of Nigeria. Licensing serves as a safeguard for consumers while ensuring businesses meet industry standards.

Globally, licensing requirements vary by country and sector. In the European Union, businesses dealing with chemicals must comply with the Registration, Evaluation, Authorization, and Restriction of Chemicals (REACH) regulation to ensure safety and environmental protection. Similarly, in the United States, the Food and Drug Administration (FDA) regulates food, drugs, and medical devices, requiring businesses to obtain approval before entering the market. Understanding and fulfilling licensing requirements not only ensure compliance but also enhance credibility and consumer trust.

Contracts are another indispensable element of establishing a business legally. A well-drafted contract serves as a blueprint for business relationships, outlining the rights, responsibilities, and expectations of all parties involved. Contracts protect businesses from misunderstandings and legal disputes, providing a framework for resolving disagreements. Whether it's a lease agreement, employment contract, or supplier agreement, ensuring contracts are comprehensive and enforceable is vital. Depending on the locality, contracts are governed by common law principles, and their enforceability often depends on clarity, legality, and the inclusion of all necessary elements such as offer, acceptance, consideration, and intention to create legal relations.

The global importance of contracts cannot be overstated. In the United Kingdom, contracts are similarly governed by common law, emphasizing the need for clear terms and conditions. In countries like Japan, cultural factors play a significant role in contract negotiations, where emphasis is placed on mutual understanding and trust before formal agreements are signed. Entrepreneurs must adapt to the legal and cultural nuances of the regions they operate in while ensuring their contracts are robust and protective.

Another critical aspect of laying a legal foundation is intellectual property (IP) protection. In a competitive business landscape, safeguarding innovations, brands, and creative works is essential. Individuals can protect trademarks, patents, and copyrights through registration with the Nigerian Copyright Commission or the Ministry of Industry, Trade, and Investment. Trademarks protect brand identity, while patents safeguard inventions, and copyrights protect artistic and literary works. Failing to protect intellectual property exposes businesses to the risk of theft or misuse, potentially undermining their competitive advantage.

The relevance of IP protection extends far beyond Nigeria. Globally, countries like the United States and China have robust IP protection frameworks, reflecting the importance of innovation-driven economies. In the European Union, the European Patent Office provides patent protection across member states, streamlining the process for entrepreneurs seeking to expand internationally. Regardless of location, investing in IP protection is a strategic move that fosters innovation and long-term business growth.

Navigating taxation is another essential aspect of establishing a business legally. Founders must understand their tax obligations to avoid penalties and maintain financial stability. In Nigeria, businesses are subject to various taxes, including value-added tax (VAT), corporate income tax, and personal income tax for sole proprietors and partnerships. Registering with the Federal Inland Revenue Service (FIRS) is mandatory to obtain a Tax Identification Number (TIN), which is required for tax compliance. Keeping accurate financial records and filing tax returns on time are crucial practices for maintaining compliance and avoiding disputes with tax authorities.

Similarly, global tax systems emphasize compliance and record-keeping. In the United States, businesses must adhere to federal, state, and local tax laws, which vary significantly by jurisdiction. The Internal Revenue Service (IRS) provides guidelines and resources to help entrepreneurs navigate the complex tax landscape. In developing economies, efforts are being made to simplify tax systems and encourage compliance among small and medium-sized enterprises. Regardless of the system, understanding and fulfilling tax obligations is a cornerstone of legal business operations.

Finally, establishing a business legally requires proactive measures to stay informed about evolving laws and regulations. Legal frameworks are dynamic, reflecting changes in economic conditions, societal needs, and technological advancements. Entrepreneurs must invest in legal counsel or leverage technology to stay updated on regulatory changes that could impact their operations. This proactive approach ensures compliance and positions the business to adapt effectively to new challenges and opportunities. Laying a solid legal foundation is a fundamental step in building a successful business. From choosing the right structure and registering with authorities to securing licenses, drafting contracts, and protecting intellectual property, every aspect plays a critical role in ensuring compliance and safeguarding interests. Founders, whether in Nigeria or elsewhere, must approach the legal aspects of their business with diligence and foresight. By establishing their businesses legally, they not only mitigate risks but also create a platform for sustainable growth and success. Understanding the universal principles of legal compliance, while tailoring them to specific regional requirements, empowers entrepreneurs to navigate the complexities of the business world with confidence and clarity.

Staying Compliant with Regulatory Frameworks

Ensuring adherence to regulatory requirements is one of the most critical responsibilities for those venturing into business ownership. Beyond the initial legal steps of establishment, maintaining compliance is a continuous process that safeguards the organization against potential penalties, fosters trust with stakeholders, and secures long-term sustainability. For enterprises operating in dynamic environments like Nigeria, staying aligned with regulatory mandates involves a combination of vigilance, strategic planning, and adaptability. However, these principles transcend borders, as businesses worldwide must navigate unique legal landscapes while striving for ethical and operational excellence.

One of the foremost areas of compliance is taxation. Every commercial entity, regardless of its size or industry, bears a fiscal responsibility to contribute to public coffers. Businesses are required to comply with several taxation regulations, including corporate income tax, value-added tax (VAT), and personal income tax for individuals operating as sole proprietors or partners. Registering with the Federal Inland Revenue Service (FIRS) is non-negotiable, as obtaining a Tax Identification Number (TIN) is a prerequisite for conducting legitimate financial activities. Maintaining meticulous financial records and filing timely tax returns not only fulfills legal obligations but also establishes transparency, which can enhance credibility with investors and customers alike.

Globally, tax systems reflect the socio-economic priorities of their respective governments, but the principles of accuracy and timeliness remain universal. In developed markets like the United States, companies must comply with federal, state, and local tax codes, each imposing distinct requirement. Similarly, in the European Union, value-added tax systems are harmonized across member states, yet each country enforces its specific rates and rules. For startups and growing ventures, the complexity of tax compliance can seem daunting, but leveraging professional tax advisors or digital tools can streamline the process and prevent costly errors.

Compliance is not limited to taxation. Many industries are governed by sector-specific regulations designed to protect consumers, ensure safety, and uphold ethical standards. In Nigeria, for instance, businesses in the food and beverage industry must adhere to guidelines set forth by the National Agency for Food and Drug Administration and Control (NAFDAC). These rules dictate product labeling, quality assurance measures, and safety protocols. Similarly, financial service providers must comply with regulations established by the Central Bank of Nigeria (CBN), including anti-money laundering directives and capital adequacy requirements.

Industry-specific regulations extend globally, and businesses operating across borders must account for multiple jurisdictions. Technology firms handling user data must align with privacy laws such as the European Union's General Data Protection Regulation (GDPR). Non-compliance with GDPR can lead to hefty fines and reputational damage. Similarly, businesses engaging in international trade must navigate customs regulations, import-export tariffs, and trade agreements, which vary depending on geopolitical relationships. Staying informed about such regulations is essential to mitigate risks and maintain seamless operations.

Labor laws constitute another significant aspect of regulatory adherence. Treating employees fairly, providing safe working conditions, and complying with wage and hour laws are not merely legal obligations but also ethical imperatives. In Nigeria, the Labor Act outlines the minimum standards for employment contracts, working hours, and termination processes. Adhering to these provisions protects both the workforce and the employer, fostering a harmonious work environment. Beyond Nigeria, countries like Germany are known for stringent labor laws that prioritize worker welfare, including mandatory paid leave and collective bargaining rights. Understanding and respecting these laws is crucial for businesses aiming to attract top talent and maintain a positive reputation.

Environmental regulations are becoming increasingly prominent as global awareness of climate change and sustainability grows. For businesses, complying with environmental standards enforced by agencies like the National Environmental Standards and Regulations Enforcement Agency (NESREA) is essential. These regulations aim to prevent pollution, manage waste, and protect natural resources. Enterprises in sectors such as manufacturing and construction are particularly affected, as their activities often have significant environmental footprints. Globally, initiatives like the Paris Agreement and local green laws are pushing organizations to adopt eco-friendly practices, such as reducing emissions and conserving energy.

Data protection and cybersecurity laws are also gaining traction, driven by the rise of digital transformation. The Nigeria Data Protection Regulation (NDPR) outlines guidelines for collecting, processing, and storing personal data. Businesses are required to implement data security measures and obtain user consent before utilizing their information. Non-compliance not only attracts fines but also damages trust, which can be detrimental in an increasingly data-driven economy. Internationally, laws like the

California Consumer Privacy Act (CCPA) in the United States and GDPR in Europe further emphasize the importance of safeguarding customer data.

Navigating these diverse compliance requirements demands a proactive approach. Ignorance of the law is not an acceptable defense, and relying solely on hindsight can lead to irreparable consequences. Successful business owners and executives prioritize ongoing education and awareness of regulatory changes. One effective strategy is to appoint a compliance officer or establish an internal compliance team responsible for monitoring legal developments, conducting audits, and ensuring adherence to standards. In smaller organizations, outsourcing compliance functions to legal experts or consulting firms can provide the necessary expertise without the burden of maintaining an in-house team.

Technology is another powerful ally in the quest for compliance. Regulatory technology, or "RegTech," leverages digital solutions to simplify and automate compliance processes. Tools such as tax filing software, contract management platforms, and data monitoring systems can reduce the manual effort involved in staying compliant while minimizing errors. Businesses can use platforms that integrate with FIRS systems to streamline tax filings. Globally, companies are adopting artificial intelligence-powered solutions to track regulatory updates, analyze risks, and ensure adherence across multiple jurisdictions.

Establishing strong relationships with regulators is also instrumental in maintaining compliance. Open communication channels with government agencies and industry associations can provide clarity on regulatory expectations and offer opportunities for feedback. Engaging with bodies like the Nigerian Export Promotion Council (NEPC) or the Small and Medium Enterprises Development Agency of Nigeria (SMEDAN) can provide valuable resources and guidance for businesses. Similarly, in other countries, participation in trade associations or public-private dialogues fosters mutual understanding and collaboration between businesses and regulatory authorities. Another essential element of compliance is fostering a culture of integrity within the organization. Employees at all levels must understand the importance of ethical conduct and regulatory adherence. Regular training programs, clear policies, and a zero-tolerance approach to violations create an environment where compliance is viewed as a shared responsibility. This cultural alignment not only reduces the likelihood of infractions but also enhances the organization's reputation among stakeholders.

Penalties for non-compliance can range from fines and operational disruptions to reputational damage and legal battles. In extreme cases, businesses may face closure or loss of licenses, jeopardizing years of effort and investment. The consequences highlight the importance of staying vigilant and adopting a preventive mindset. Entrepreneurs and business leaders must recognize that the cost of compliance is an investment in stability and growth, whereas the cost of non-compliance can be catastrophic.

Operating a business requires more than an initial understanding of laws; it necessitates the ability to adapt to ever-changing legal landscapes. Rules, regulations, and policies evolve continuously, shaped by economic shifts, technological advancements, and societal priorities. For those leading businesses, especially in countries like Nigeria, navigating this dynamic environment demands proactive strategies and a commitment to staying ahead of the curve. Though this challenge exists universally, the specific nuances vary across regions, making adaptability a crucial skill in ensuring sustained compliance and operational success.

The nature of regulatory changes often reflects the state of governance and the priorities of a nation's policymakers. In Nigeria, for instance, evolving economic policies aimed at fostering entrepreneurship have introduced initiatives such as the Companies and Allied Matters Act (CAMA) 2020, which simplified business registration processes and introduced innovations like single-member companies. While such reforms are designed to ease the regulatory burden on enterprises, they require entrepreneurs to remain vigilant in understanding and adopting new processes. Failure to do so can result in delays, non-compliance, or missed opportunities to leverage advantages embedded in updated laws.

Globally, the regulatory environment is also influenced by technological progress. The rise of e-commerce and digital payments, for example, has led governments to institute tax reforms targeting online transactions. The introduction of digital services tax reflects a response to the growing digital economy. Similarly, international frameworks like the Organization for Economic Co-operation and Development (OECD)'s global tax reform seek to address taxation challenges posed by cross-border digital activities. Entrepreneurs venturing into tech-driven businesses must be prepared to navigate such dynamic regulatory territories, ensuring compliance while staying competitive.

Beyond taxation, the realm of environmental law has undergone rapid transformation due to global concerns about climate change and sustainability. In our locality, regulators have introduced stricter environmental standards for industries with significant ecological footprints, such as manufacturing and oil production. Businesses must now adopt greener practices and invest in technologies that reduce emissions and waste. Internationally, agreements like the Paris Climate Accord and subsequent national commitments have increased scrutiny on carbon footprints, pushing companies to rethink their operations. Adapting to these environmental regulations not only fulfills legal requirements but also aligns businesses with global sustainability trends, enhancing their appeal to environmentally conscious consumers and investors.

Labor laws are another area where legal frameworks frequently shift, reflecting changing societal norms and economic realities. Minimum wage adjustments, enhanced protections for workers, and evolving workplace safety standards are common examples. Periodic revisions of the national minimum wage require employers to adjust salary structures to comply with government mandates. Internationally, countries like the United States have witnessed debates over federal wage increases, and regions like the European Union continually refine directives aimed at improving workplace conditions. Founders must remain agile in responding to these changes, not only to avoid penalties but also to foster positive employer-employee relationships.

The pace of regulatory change is further accelerated by advancements in data and cybersecurity laws. As digital transformation spreads, businesses across the globe face stringent requirements for data protection. In Nigeria, the Nigeria Data Protection Regulation (NDPR) serves as the framework for managing personal data, emphasizing transparency, user consent, and security measures. However, the global nature of digital commerce means that Nigerian businesses serving international markets may also need to comply with foreign laws, such as the European Union's GDPR. Understanding the interplay between local and international regulations is critical for entrepreneurs looking to scale their operations across borders.

To effectively navigate these evolving landscapes, businesses must develop systems for monitoring legal updates. Depending on the scale of operations, this may involve assigning dedicated compliance officers, subscribing to legal monitoring services, or working closely with legal professionals. In Nigeria, consulting with regulatory agencies such as the Corporate Affairs Commission (CAC) or FIRS can provide clarity on recent changes. Engaging with industry associations and trade groups is also beneficial, as these bodies often serve as intermediaries between businesses and regulators, offering insights into upcoming reforms and collective advocacy.

International businesses or those aspiring to expand into foreign markets face additional layers of complexity. Navigating multinational regulations requires a deep understanding of cross-border laws and trade agreements. For instance, a Nigerian export-oriented business must comply with local customs regulations while aligning with international standards governing product quality, labeling, and shipping. Entrepreneurs operating in such contexts often benefit from partnerships with legal advisors specializing in international trade or membership in global trade associations that provide guidance on navigating regulatory frameworks across different jurisdictions.

A forward-thinking approach to compliance also involves scenario planning and risk management. Persons should anticipate potential regulatory changes by staying attuned to economic, political, and societal trends. As global momentum grows toward decarbonization, industries reliant on fossil fuels are likely to face tighter restrictions. Businesses in such sectors must proactively explore alternative energy sources, redesign products, or diversify revenue streams to mitigate risks. Conducting periodic risk assessments and aligning strategies with anticipated regulatory trends not only ensures readiness but also positions businesses as leaders in innovation and responsibility.

Moreover, engaging with regulators in constructive dialogue can influence the regulatory landscape in ways that benefit businesses and society alike. Founders can participate in consultations, provide feedback on proposed regulations, and advocate for reforms that balance economic growth with societal goals. Platforms such as public hearings organized by government agencies or chambers of commerce provide opportunities for businesses to voice their perspectives. Collaborating with other entrepreneurs and forming coalitions can amplify the impact of such advocacy efforts.

Non-compliance with evolving regulations can have severe consequences, ranging from fines and legal disputes to reputational damage and operational disruptions. In extreme cases, businesses may face closure or be barred from certain markets. These risks underscore the importance of adaptability in maintaining compliance. Entrepreneurs must view regulatory challenges not as obstacles but as opportunities to innovate, differentiate, and build resilience.

Adapting to changing legal and regulatory environments is an essential aspect of running a successful enterprise. Whether dealing with taxation, labor laws, environmental standards, or data protection regulations, staying compliant requires vigilance, strategic planning, and a willingness to embrace change. By leveraging technology, fostering organizational learning, and engaging with regulators, entrepreneurs can navigate these complexities with confidence.

CHAPTER TWELVE
WELLNESS AND BALANCE: THRIVING WITHOUT BURNOUT

We have described entrepreneurship with various words, and it is often portrayed as an exhilarating and fulfilling journey, filled with the promise of growth, innovation, and success. However, this path can be overwhelming, especially when the pressures of building and managing a business begin to take a toll on one's personal well-being. Burnout is a hidden epidemic among entrepreneurs, one that can gradually creep up on individuals without their awareness until it's too late. Recognizing the signs of burnout is the first crucial step in preventing it from hindering both personal health and business success.

Burnout is not merely a result of being overworked; it's a state of emotional, mental, and physical exhaustion caused by prolonged stress, often brought on by excessive demands placed on an individual. In the context of entrepreneurship, burnout can manifest in many forms, including chronic fatigue, feelings of inadequacy, and a pervasive sense of being overwhelmed. When individuals become immersed in their ventures, often working long hours and managing multiple roles, the constant drive to succeed can gradually undermine their ability to maintain a healthy work-life balance.

One of the key indicators of burnout is physical exhaustion. Persons may feel physically drained despite getting enough sleep. This fatigue isn't just a sign of physical overexertion but rather it's often linked to stress and emotional depletion. Entrepreneurs may find themselves waking up tired, struggling to focus, and lacking the energy required to manage even the simplest of tasks. Over time, this physical fatigue builds up, making it difficult to maintain productivity or enthusiasm for the business. Another prominent sign of burnout is emotional exhaustion. Persons often start their ventures with a deep sense of passion, enthusiasm, and a strong belief in their mission. However, when burnout sets in, this passion starts to fade, leaving behind a feeling of emotional emptiness. Entrepreneurs may find themselves feeling detached from their business or frustrated with tasks they once enjoyed. Their passion for their product, team, or customers diminishes, and they may struggle to connect with the purpose behind their work. This emotional disconnection can lead to feelings of frustration, disappointment, and a lack of motivation.

The impact of burnout on one's emotional state can also lead to anxiety and depression. These emotional symptoms can exacerbate the exhaustion felt by the person, creating a vicious cycle that makes it even harder to break free. Entrepreneurs may feel trapped in their business, believing that if they stop, everything will fall apart. This belief can drive them to push even harder, leading to even greater burnout.

Cognitive fatigue is another sign of burnout that can severely impact an entrepreneur's performance. The inability to focus, make decisions, and solve problems effectively is a common symptom of burnout. Persons may find themselves forgetting critical details, missing deadlines, or making errors that they wouldn't typically make. Their ability to think creatively and strategically may diminish, leaving them feeling stuck in their business operations. This lack of mental clarity can have a profound impact on the overall success of the business, as strategic decisions become increasingly difficult to make.

Besides cognitive challenges, entrepreneurs experiencing burnout often report feelings of isolation and a loss of connection with others. As they become consumed by their business, they may begin to withdraw from personal relationships, social gatherings, and professional networks. The weight of responsibility can feel isolating, and individuals may feel as though they are carrying the burden of their business alone. This sense of isolation can further exacerbate feelings of stress, leading to a downward spiral of burnout.

Physical symptoms also often accompany burnout. Entrepreneurs may experience headaches, sleep disturbances, digestive issues, or increased susceptibility to illness. These symptoms are often overlooked or dismissed as minor inconveniences, but they are powerful indicators that the body is under chronic stress. Over time, these physical manifestations can compound the mental and emotional effects of burnout, leading to even greater health concerns.

Recognizing the signs of burnout is particularly challenging because they often develop gradually over time. Entrepreneurs are conditioned to push through difficulties, believing that hard work and perseverance will eventually lead to success. However, ignoring the warning signs of burnout can have serious long-term consequences, both for the individual and the business. They may find themselves unable to perform at their best, leading to lower productivity, strained relationships, and a lack of satisfaction with their work.

There are also distinct differences between stress and burnout that are important to understand. Stress is a temporary reaction to a specific challenge or situation, and it can be managed with proper coping mechanisms such as time management, delegation, or relaxation techniques. Burnout, on the other hand, is a deeper and more chronic condition that affects the entrepreneur's entire mindset and ability to function effectively. While stress may come and go, burnout requires a long-term approach to recovery and prevention.

Entrepreneurs, particularly in fast-paced and competitive environments, may feel pressure to push themselves to their limits in order to succeed. However, the reality is that unchecked burnout can have devastating consequences on their health, relationships, and overall business performance. Recognizing the signs of burnout early on is critical to maintaining balance and achieving long-term success. While burnout can affect anyone, certain factors make entrepreneurs particularly vulnerable. The responsibility of running a business, the pressure to innovate and compete, the need to constantly hustle, and the emotional investment in the venture can all contribute to burnout. They often feel like they must do everything themselves whether it's managing finances, overseeing operations, handling customer service, or marketing the product. The overwhelming nature of these tasks, compounded by the emotional and physical exhaustion of working long hours, can quickly lead to burnout.

In Nigeria, for example, the entrepreneurial landscape is both challenging and rewarding. Entrepreneurs often face a range of obstacles, such as regulatory hurdles, unreliable infrastructure, and limited access to funding. These factors can lead to high levels of stress, which can easily transform into burnout. The drive to succeed in such an environment can be exhausting, and many Nigerian entrepreneurs may not immediately recognize the toll it takes on their mental and physical well-being. The pressure to overcome adversity and achieve success can cause many to work tirelessly, pushing them through exhaustion until they experience the full effects of burnout.

Globally, burnout is becoming an increasingly recognized issue. In the United States, the World Health Organization (WHO) has officially recognized burnout as an occupational phenomenon, acknowledging the growing need to address mental health in the workplace. Similarly, in Europe, there has been a rise in corporate wellness programs designed to combat burnout and promote work-life balance. Entrepreneurs worldwide are beginning to realize that the key to success is not working harder but working smarter and maintaining a sustainable pace that allows them to continue performing at their best.

Preventing this occurrence requires a shift in mindset. Founders need to embrace the idea that self-care is not a luxury, but a necessity for sustained success. This mindset shift involves recognizing the importance of taking breaks, seeking support, and delegating tasks to ensure that the entrepreneur's energy is not depleted over time. Rather than pushing through the exhaustion, entrepreneurs need to listen to their bodies and minds, taking proactive steps to prioritize wellness and balance.

Burnout is a silent and gradual process that affects the emotional, physical, and cognitive aspects of an individual's life. Entrepreneurs who fail to recognize the early warning signs may find themselves in a state of emotional and mental exhaustion, which can undermine their productivity, creativity, and overall business success. By identifying the symptoms of burnout and taking proactive steps to address them, entrepreneurs can ensure that they not only survive but thrive in their ventures.

As entrepreneurs, the quest for success often leads to an intense, high-paced work environment where every day feels like a race against the clock. The drive to grow the business and the desire to stay competitive can make it easy to lose sight of the need for balance and self-care. This is where the importance of building sustainable work habits comes into play. Developing strategies that allow for sustained productivity without overexertion is key to thriving in the long run, both professionally and personally. Persons who establish strong, healthy work habits can create an environment that supports growth without the risk of burnout.

The foundation of sustainable work habits begins with understanding the concept of balance and time management. Entrepreneurs often wear multiple hats, from managing day-to-day operations to strategizing for the future. The temptation to juggle it all without pause is overwhelming. However, adopting a balanced approach means recognizing that personal well-being is just as important as business success. Sustainable work habits are rooted in a long-term perspective, rather than the short-term hustle that is often glorified in entrepreneurial circles.

A powerful tool in building sustainable work habits is effective time management. Entrepreneurs who fail to manage their time well often find themselves overwhelmed, leading to burnout. Effective time management involves organizing one's tasks, prioritizing what truly matters, and being disciplined about how time is spent. Persons can use tools such as to-do lists, project management software, or simple time-blocking techniques to help structure their workday. Time-blocking, for example, involves setting aside specific periods of time for specific tasks whether it's working on a project, responding to emails, or taking a break. This method ensures that no task is neglected, while also creating a clear boundary between work and personal time.

While time management helps allocate the necessary time for work, it's equally important to prioritize tasks. Founders often face an endless list of responsibilities, many of which can feel urgent. However, not every task requires immediate attention. The ability to discern between what is truly urgent and what can be delayed or delegated is critical to avoiding burnout. Entrepreneurs can apply the Eisenhower Matrix, a time management tool that divides tasks into four quadrants based on urgency and importance. Tasks that are both urgent and important should be tackled immediately, while tasks that are neither urgent nor important can be eliminated or delegated. This process helps them focus on what will drive their business forward, rather than getting caught up in less impactful activities.

Delegation is another key practice that contributes to building sustainable work habits. As entrepreneurs grow their businesses, they often take on too much themselves, fearing that they are the only ones who can do certain tasks. However, this mindset can quickly lead to exhaustion and inefficiency. Delegating tasks to a trusted team allows you to free up time for higher-level strategic decisions while empowering your employees or partners to take ownership of important responsibilities. Effective delegation requires trust and clear communication. Entrepreneurs must ensure that the people they delegate to are equipped with the right tools, resources, and authority to execute tasks successfully.

Another critical aspect is setting boundaries. As an entrepreneur, the line between personal time and work time can easily blur. Many people feel compelled to respond to emails, take phone calls, or complete work late into the night. However, the constant availability can lead to mental and physical exhaustion. Setting boundaries means defining clear times when work is allowed and when it should be put aside in favor of personal activities, rest, and relaxation. This also extends to setting expectations with clients, employees, and business partners. Entrepreneurs must communicate that, while they are dedicated to the success of the business, they are also committed to their well-being and personal life.

An effective work-life balance is not just about setting boundaries and managing time; it also involves taking regular breaks throughout the day. Research shows that frequent breaks can enhance productivity, creativity, and overall well-being. Entrepreneurs who push themselves without taking time for rest may experience diminishing returns as they continue to work through fatigue. Incorporating short, intentional breaks can rejuvenate the mind, improve focus, and prevent the buildup of stress. Breaks can range from a five-minute stretch to a 30-minute walk or a short meditation session. These moments of respite are essential for recharging and maintaining high performance throughout the day.

It is also imperative that one should also ensure that they get sufficient sleep. The culture of late-night hustling may lead some entrepreneurs to sacrifice sleep, believing that working around the clock will lead to success. However, research consistently shows that adequate rest is crucial for cognitive function, decision-making, and emotional regulation. Founders who neglect their sleep risk making poor decisions, losing their creativity, and damaging their overall health. Sustainable work habits involve respecting the need for rest and creating a routine that prioritizes quality sleep.

Physical health is another pillar of sustainable work habits. Persons who neglect their physical well-being may find themselves depleted and less effective at managing their business. Regular exercise, a balanced diet, and staying hydrated all play an essential role in maintaining energy levels and mental clarity. Physical health directly impacts how entrepreneurs perform in their businesses. For instance, exercise is proven to reduce stress, enhance mood, and boost focus, all of which are critical for entrepreneurs to perform at their best. Developing a routine that includes time for physical activity can help maintain stamina for the long haul.

Mindfulness is another practice that can support this concept. You can use mindfulness techniques such as meditation or deep-breathing exercises to manage stress and maintain mental clarity. These practices help entrepreneurs remain present, focused, and balanced throughout the day, especially when juggling multiple tasks. Mindfulness has been shown to improve emotional regulation, decrease anxiety, and increase productivity, making it a valuable tool in an entrepreneur's repertoire. Regular mindfulness practice can also help persons stay connected to their values, ensuring that their decisions align with both personal and professional goals. Maintaining social connections and seeking support is equally important for sustaining healthy work habits. Entrepreneurs often face the challenge of isolation, especially if they are building a business on their own. Loneliness can lead to stress and burnout, which can undermine overall well-being. Building a network of supportive colleagues, mentors, and friends provides a safety net and offers an outlet for expressing frustrations and seeking advice. Persons should cultivate relationships both within and outside their industry, as these connections can provide emotional support, new perspectives, and valuable guidance.

The importance of mental health cannot be overstated in the context of building sustainable work habits. Mental health issues, such as anxiety and depression, can have a profound effect on an entrepreneur's ability to function effectively. Persons should prioritize their mental health by seeking professional help when necessary and by cultivating habits that support mental well-being, such as journaling, talking to loved ones, or engaging in creative activities. A healthy mind allows entrepreneurs to make sound decisions, maintain focus, and build strength in the face of challenges.

Health and well-being are often overlooked in the pursuit of entrepreneurial success. Many business owners find themselves caught in an unrelenting cycle of long hours, high stress, and limited personal time, believing that this sacrifice is the price of success. However, neglecting physical health, mental well-being, and emotional resilience can undermine even the most promising ventures. Integrating health and wellness into the entrepreneurial journey is not merely a personal priority but it is a strategic imperative that enhances decision-making.

As entrepreneurship continues to evolve in an increasingly demanding world, the integration of health and well-being into the journey is no longer optional rather than is essential. By prioritizing their physical health, nurturing their mental well-being, fostering social connections, and creating supportive workplace cultures, entrepreneurs can achieve success that is not only sustainable but also deeply fulfilling.

Thriving without burnout is possible when health becomes an integral part of the equation, empowering business leaders to excel in their endeavors while enjoying the journey along the way.

CONCLUSION

Answering the Question—So You Want to Be an entrepreneur?

As we reach the final pages of, *So You Want to Be an entrepreneur?* It's time to pause and reflect on the expedition we've undertaken together. Starting and running a business is not a path for everyone, and that's perfectly okay. The beauty of asking yourself this question lies in the process of uncovering your core motivations, comprehending the realities of building a business, and making an informed decision about whether this challenging yet rewarding endeavor aligns with your personal goals and values.

Throughout these chapters, we've explored various facets of the business world, its thrilling opportunities and inevitable challenges. From discovering your "why" as a founder to crafting an enterprise that endures, we've delved into the mindsets, strategies, and practicalities required to thrive. We've examined the lessons learned from failures, the importance of legal and financial preparedness, the delicate art of scaling effectively, and the transformative impact of giving back to society. Alongside global insights, you've also encountered examples that highlight the untapped ingenuity in regions like Africa, particularly Nigeria, which continues to inspire innovation on multiple fronts.

But the core of building a venture goes beyond strategies or blueprints. It's deeply personal. It's about your vision, resilience, and commitment to adapting and growing amid uncertainty. It's about crafting something meaningful that reflects your values and aspirations. Most importantly, it's about solving problems, creating value, and leaving a legacy that touches lives far beyond your own.

As you close this book, the question remains: Do you want to embrace the life of a creator and leader in business? If your answer is yes, then embrace this opportunity with a clear perspective and a sense of purpose. Carry forward the lessons you've learned here and use them to guide your business journey. Build something that not only achieves success but also mirrors your identity and the change you want to bring to the world.

If your answer is no that, too, is an accomplishment. Understanding that this path isn't your calling is a sign of strength and self-awareness. The principles, skills, and insights shared in this book can still empower you in whatever professional field you choose, helping you add value and make meaningful contributions.

Ultimately, pursuing a business venture isn't just about starting companies or creating products rather it's about adopting a mindset of problem-solving, innovation, and resilience. Whether you decide to take this path or apply these principles elsewhere, the ideas explored here remind us of the importance of dreaming big, acting decisively, and staying authentic in the face of challenges.

The world needs creators, leaders, and visionaries. It needs individuals who can challenge norms and carve out new opportunities. If you decide to answer the call of business leadership, remember that the road ahead will demand effort and determination, but the rewards including personal growth, impact, and fulfillment will make the pursuit worthwhile.

Now, it's up to you. Take the insights you've gained, assess the possibilities, and make your choice. Whether or not you choose to embark on this path let this book serve as a reminder that every great outcome starts with asking the right questions and committing to thoughtful answers. Whatever you decide, make your decision boldly, and let it be one that brings you closer to your goals and your best self.

Essential Resources for Aspiring Entrepreneurs

Reading widely is one of the most effective ways to deepen your understanding of entrepreneurship and gain new perspectives. The entrepreneurial world is vast, and learning from the experiences, theories, and advice of others can help you make more informed decisions on whether this path is right for you. Here, I suggest 10 essential books authored by thought leaders and innovators from around the globe, providing diverse insights to guide your exploration.

The Lean Startup by Eric Ries (United States)

This book redefined how startups approach growth and innovation. Ries introduces the concept of building minimum viable products (MVPs) and emphasizes learning quickly through experimentation. The Lean Startup offers practical advice on navigating uncertainty, which is invaluable for anyone considering launching a business.

Zero to One: Notes on Startups, or How to Build the Future by Peter Thiel with Blake Masters (United States)

Co-founder of PayPal, Peter Thiel challenges conventional thinking and encourages entrepreneurs to create something entirely new. This book explores the concept of monopoly-driven innovation and the importance of thinking differently. It's an eye-opener for those who want to assess whether they have a unique vision for their venture.

Start with Why: How Great Leaders Inspire Everyone to Take Action by Simon Sinek (United Kingdom)

Sinek explores the idea of purpose, helping readers understand the importance of finding their "why." For aspiring entrepreneurs, this book is essential to identifying the core motivations driving their desire to start a business and how they can communicate their purpose to inspire others.

The Hard Thing About Hard Things: Building a Business When There Are No Easy Answers by Ben Horowitz (United States)

In this non-nonsense guide, Ben Horowitz offers a raw and honest account of the challenges of running a business. The book provides practical advice on making difficult decisions, managing crises, and leading teams through uncertainty, lessons that every prospective entrepreneur should learn early.

Dare to Lead: Brave Work. Tough Conversations. Whole Hearts. by Brené Brown (United States)

Brené Brown's work focuses on vulnerability, courage, and leadership, offering insights into the emotional resilience needed to succeed. Aspiring entrepreneurs will benefit from her lessons on creating authentic connections and leading with purpose and integrity.

The Alchemist by Paulo Coelho (Brazil)

Though not a traditional business book, Coelho's global bestseller is a fable about pursuing dreams and finding purpose. Its universal themes resonate with anyone at a crossroads in life, including those deciding whether to embrace the entrepreneurial journey.

How to Avoid a Climate Disaster: The Solutions We Have and the Breakthroughs We Need by Bill Gates (United States)

Gates combines a global perspective with actionable insights into tackling the world's biggest challenges. Aspiring entrepreneurs interested in creating businesses with a social or environmental impact will find inspiration and guidance in this forward-thinking book.

African Entrepreneurs: 50 Success Stories edited by Miatta Fahnbulleh (Liberia)

This compilation highlights the journeys of 50 African entrepreneurs, showcasing their innovative solutions to local and global challenges. It provides invaluable inspiration for anyone seeking examples of how to thrive in often-overlooked markets, particularly in Africa.

Ikigai: The Japanese Secret to a Long and Happy Life by Héctor García and Francesc Miralles (Japan/Spain)

Drawing on Japanese philosophy, this book explores the concept of "ikigai", a sense of purpose that gives life meaning. It encourages readers to align their passions, skills, and societal contributions, a critical consideration for anyone contemplating entrepreneurship.

Rework by Jason Fried and David Heinemeier Hansson (Denmark/United States)

This unconventional book challenges traditional business wisdom, offering a simpler approach to starting and running a venture. It's an excellent read for entrepreneurs who want to embrace a minimalist mindset and focus on what truly matters in building a successful business.

The Billionaire's Apprentice: The Rise of the Indian American Elite and the Fall of a Silicon Valley Tycoon by Anita Raghavan (India/USA)

While not an African book, this story provides fascinating insights into the world of tech entrepreneurship and the dynamics of growing a business internationally. For African entrepreneurs, especially those exploring global markets, this book offers valuable lessons in navigating the complexities of business partnerships, ethics, and scaling.

The Smart Money Woman by Arese Ugwu (Nigeria)

Arese Ugwu's book is a personal finance guide tailored to Nigerian women, offering insights on how to make informed financial decisions and build wealth. Though focused on financial literacy, it's particularly valuable for aspiring female entrepreneurs looking to understand how to handle their business finances, scale smartly, and build a sustainable venture in an African context.

The African Entrepreneur: A Journey of Self-Discovery by Uchechi I. Eke (Nigeria)

Uchechi I. Eke's book explores the journey of African entrepreneurs, offering practical advice, anecdotes, and personal reflections. It emphasizes the importance of self-discovery in business and provides actionable insights for navigating the challenges specific to the African market. This is a great resource for those looking to create sustainable businesses in the African context.

Born to Be a Global Entrepreneur: The Success Story of Nigeria's Top Entrepreneurs by Francis O. O. Ogundele (Nigeria)

This book takes an in-depth look at the success stories of top Nigerian entrepreneurs and provides critical lessons on how they achieved success in a competitive environment. It offers practical strategies for navigating the unique obstacles in Nigeria, such as economic instability and regulatory challenges, making it highly relevant for anyone considering entrepreneurship in Nigeria or similar markets.

The Lean Startup in Africa by Andrew H. H. Waha (Kenya)

Andrew H. H. Waha explores how the Lean Startup methodology can be applied in African markets, providing tailored advice for entrepreneurs in Africa. The book covers the unique challenges faced by startups in Africa, such as access to capital, infrastructure, and local market dynamics, making it an essential guide for those looking to innovate and build businesses in the region.

www.ingramcontent.com/pod-product-compliance
Lightning Source LLC
LaVergne TN
LVHW092007090526
838202LV00001B/28